ISBN 978-0-282-21103-5
PIBN 10844560

1 MONTH OF
FREE
READING

at

www.ForgottenBooks.com

By purchasing this book you are eligible for one month membership to ForgottenBooks.com, giving you unlimited access to our entire collection of over 700,000 titles via our web site and mobile apps.

To claim your free month visit:
www.forgottenbooks.com/free844560

English
Français
Deutsche
Italiano
Español
Português

www.forgottenbooks.com

Mythology Photography **Fiction**
Fishing Christianity **Art** Cooking
Essays Buddhism Freemasonry
Medicine **Biology** Music **Ancient**
Egypt Evolution Carpentry Physics
Dance Geology **Mathematics** Fitness
Shakespeare **Folklore** Yoga Marketing
Confidence Immortality Biographies
Poetry **Psychology** Witchcraft
Electronics Chemistry History **Law**
Accounting **Philosophy** Anthropology
Alchemy Drama Quantum Mechanics
Atheism Sexual Health **Ancient History**
Entrepreneurship Languages Sport
Paleontology Needlework Islam
Metaphysics Investment Archaeology
Parenting Statistics Criminology
Motivational

A

SPECIMEN

OF

PERSIAN POETRY;

OR

ODES, OF HAFEZ: *or Hafiz*

WITH AN

ENGLISH TRANSLATION AND PARAPHRASE,

CHIEFLY FROM THE SPECIMEN POESEOS PERSICÆ OF

BARON REVIZKY,

ENVOY FROM THE EMPEROR OF GERMANY TO THE COURT OF POLAND.

WITH

HISTORICAL AND GRAMMATICAL ILLUSTRATIONS, AND A COMPLETE
ANALYSIS, FOR THE ASSISTANCE OF THOSE WHO WISH TO STUDY
THE PERSIAN LANGUAGE.

BY JOHN RICHARDSON, F.S.A.

A NEW EDITION, REVISED, CORRECTED, AND ENLARGED,
BY S. ROUSSEAU, TEACHER OF THE PERSIAN LANGUAGE.

London

PRINTED BY AND FOR THE EDITOR, WOOD STREET, SPA FIELDS;
J. SEWELL, CORNHILL; MURRAY AND HIGHLEY, FLEET STREET; AND
J. DEBRETT, PICCADILLY.
1802.

ADVERTISEMENT.

THE following work was originally publiſhed by Mr. RICHARDSON in 1774, but at that time the ſtudy of the Perſian language was not conſidered of that vaſt importance which it has ſince been found to be, to thoſe gentlemen who had occaſion to reſide in the Honourable Company's ſettlements in Hindooſtân, either in a civil or a military capacity; but on their arrival in that country, they immediately perceived they had been greatly miſtaken, and that no tranſaction or negociation of conſequence could poſſibly take place, or be carried on, without a knowledge of the court language of that extenſive empire. They were therefore compelled, before they could enter on the duties of their functions, ſo as to acquit themſelves like men, and give that ſatisfaction to their employers which every honeſt perſon feels a peculiar pleaſure in doing, to apply to a native moonſhee for aſſiſtance in the acquirement of that neceſſary tongue, which

they

they had neglected before they quitted the shores of Britain. In consequence of this infatuation, this pamphlet was long neglected ; but when by length of years the few copies that had been taken of it became scattered among the libraries of the curious, and it was not to be obtained without difficulty, it was sought for with avidity. There not being a grammatical praxis of this nature has been long cause of regret; and those gentlemen who have studied Sir William Jones's Grammar, have universally lamented, that their labours were rendered extremely tedious by the want of an analytical work, like that which is now again presented to the public. It remains only to say, that it is printed in a size proper to bind with that Gentleman's Grammar, which, by the addition of this Praxis, will be rendered doubly useful.

The Editor cannot but return his grateful thanks to the Rev. Mr. WESTON, author of " A Specimen of the Conformity of the European Languages, particularly the English, with the Oriental Languages, especially the Persian," for his very friendly communication of several excellent Notes which embellish the various pages of the following Work.

THE EDITOR.

PREFACE.

THE commerce and politics of Great Britain are now so intimately connected with those of Hindoſtan, that every important change in that great empire muſt be highly intereſting to this kingdom.

Among all the arrangements, ſuggeſted by the wiſdom of parliament, for the government of our ſettlements in thoſe diſtant regions, few perhaps could have had more ſalutary conſequences, though none has been leſs attended to, than the encouragement of the ſtudy of the languages of princes with whom we muſt treat, people with whom me muſt trade, ſubjects whom we muſt govern.

That the languages of a country where a man reſides, and with whoſe natives he has much intercourſe, are highly important to him, is a poſition unneceſſary to be inforced, becauſe univerſally admitted; nor is the concluſion leſs obvious, that if ſuch knowledge is to the higheſt degree uſeful to individuals, how much more conſequential muſt it be to the repreſentatives of a great commercial body, whom a revolution unparallelled in the annals of any nation has placed as ſovereigns over countries extenſive, populous,

and.

and rich. So circumftanced, however, to ftill be under
the neceffity, in every tranfaction of moment with the
powers of thofe countries, to correfpond and converfe
with them by the intermediation of interpreters, whofe
ignorance perhaps is only to be equalled by their perfidy,
is not only tedious, indecifive, and dangerous, but ill-fuited
to the dignity of Britain, as a powerful and learned nation.

To enlarge on the innumerable inconveniences to which the
Eaft India Company have been often expofed from the too general ignorance of their fervants, in the languages of Hindoftan, and on the dangerous neceffity arifing from thence of em-
ploying the natives in negociations of the greateft fecrecy and
importance, would be idle, becaufe lamented by many of the
moft able writers on India affairs, and confirmed by every
gentleman who has returned from thofe countries. The
frauds which accident has difcovered in the department of
revenue afford ftrong prefumption that many more have been
committed undetected; and the treachery of Poniapah, interpreter to General Lawrence *, is fufficient, were there no
other

* A particular account of the military life of this gentleman may be found fcattered
through the pages of Orme's " Hiftory of the Military Tranfactions of the Britifh
Nation in Indoftan." By the conqueft of Pondicherry, and the defence of Tritchi-
noply, General Lawrence reduced the power of the French in the Eaft, and paved
the way for one of the richeft empires that every a trading people afpired to command.
A very fuperb monument to his memory was erected at the expence of the Honourable

other examples, to set in the strongest light the danger to which their affairs have been in a variety of circumstances subjected from this cause alone*.

To guard against treachery, therefore, in negociation and war, and against fraud in revenue and commerce, are surely objects of the first magnitude, but which never will be accomplished till English gentlemen can officiate as their own

nourable East India Company in Westminster Abbey; on the top of which is an admirable bust of the General, to which the Genius of the Company is pointing, while Fame is declaring his noble exploits, at the same time holding in her hand a shield, on which is written,

> " For discipline established,
> Fortresses protected,
> Settlements extended,
> French
> And Indian armies
> defeated,
> And peace concluded
> in the Carnatic."

Close under the bust is written,

> " Born March 6, 1697.
> Died
> Jan. 10, 1775."

On a tablet of beautiful marble in relief is represented the siege of a great city, and under it the word " TRITCHINOPOLY." EDIT.

* See Orme's History, p. 350; [or 2nd edition, vol. II. p. 348, &c.] The story is long: the editor will only transcribe therefore the inference with which this elegant and intelligent writer concludes; " This complicated treachery shews to what dangers the affairs of Europeans in Hindostan may be exposed by not having persons of their own nation sufficiently versed in the languages of India to serve instead of the natives as interpreters."

inter-

interpreters; for, with people, whose leading principle is circumvention, the greatest severity of punishment* will never effectually deter, where the object is important enough to invite to treachery, where the chance of impunity is superior to that of detection, and where successful villainy is no impeachment of character.

The want of knowledge however in the Persian, the great court language of India, ought by no means to be imputed either to the want of ability or inclination in our gentlemen abroad, many men of the best parts and good education having filled with applause the various departments in India; but, though fully sensible of the high importance of the study, they have found the difficulties arising from the want of dictionaries† and other introductory books so great

and

---

* Poniapah was blown from the mouth of a cannon.

† Four years are now elapsed [this work was originally published in 1774] since the editor of this publication conceived the design of publishing Meninski's Thesaurus with an English translation, and other improvements. He communicated the plan to William Jones, Esq. then at Spa, who on the most liberal principles engaged in the superintendance of the work. To give a history of the zeal and assiduity with which this great object was pursued though inconceivable difficulties and disappointments, would be extremely uninteresting to the reader; it is only necessary to say, that though the list of subscribers in point of quality was extremely flattering, yet the *sang froid* with which it was viewed by the Public at large made him at length, after much loss and more labour, reluctantly listen to the voice of prudence, and desist from an undertaking which, from the vast expence and inadequate encouragement, promised to recompense but fatigue and loss of fortune, seasoned perhaps with that ridicule, and censure, which men of confined ideas

will

and infurmountable, that they have been difcouraged, and defifted from the purfuit.   In

will ever liberally beftow on every undertaking, how deferving foever, which
does not prove fuccefsful.

Another plan on a lefs complicated and lefs extenfive fcale, however, appearing
to be wifhed for by fome of the directors of the honourable Eaft India Company,
the editor, in confequence, prefented a fpecimen to the court, which met with ap-
probation ; but the affairs of the Company being by this time under the confideration of Parliament, they could not afford that affiftance which in other circumftances
they would moft readily have granted : they were pleafed however to fubfcribe for
One hundred Copies, and to recommend it, by a minute of Court, to every perfon going out in their fervice to India.

Candour makes it neceffary further to add, that many years having now been loft,
from the want of that encouragement neceffary to infure fuccefs to an undertaking
fo arduous and laborious, Mr. Jones has in the mean time been called to the Bar, to
the duties of which he propofes now to dedicate his whole attention : having therefore taken his final leave of Eaftern learning, he will not now be induced to employ
any part of his time in an active concern in any work relative to thofe languages *.

The principles of the new plan will be laid before the Public on or before the
16th of May, when the Editor refpectfully requefts that fuch of the original fub-
fcribers to Meninfki as incline to withdraw, would fend their receipts, in order
that the fubfcriptions may be returned †.

* That fuch was the refolution of Sir William Jones, every perfon converfant in Oriental literature muft be well aware, fince himfelf made the declaration in a note at
the clofe of the Preface to the after editions of his Grammar ; and fuch was his inten-
tion ; but being appointed to go to the Eaft in a judicial capacity, he renewed his Oriental refearches with redoubled ardour and fuccefs, a fufficient teftimony of which
may be found in the excellent fpeeches he delivered to the Afiatic Society (of which he
was the founder and the prefident, until death put a period to his ufeful labours,)
and which, with many other of his papers, are printed in the Afiatic Refearches ; at
prefent confifting of fix volumes 4to and 8vo, which every Orientalift ought to have
in his poffeffion. EDIT.

† This laborious work at length appeared in two large volumes folio under the title of
" A Dictionary Perfian, Arabic, and Englifh, by John Richardfon, of the Middle Tem-
ple, and Fellow of Wadham College, Oxford." The firft volume was publifhed in
1777, and the fecond in 1780. The original price was ten pounds; but, owing to
the trifling encouragement given to Oriental literature, many of the copies remained
on the fhelves of the bookfellers till within thefe few years, when by its being generally underftood that a knowledge of the Perfian language was abfolutely neceffary for
every gentleman whofe avocations require his refidence in Hindoftan, the work at
length became fcarce, and in 1800 arofe to the aftonifhing fum of thirty guineas per
copy. This, however, has been fince obviated by a company of enterprifing bookfellers, who reprinted great part of the work, and reduced it to fixteen guineas, its prefent value. EDIT.

In fuch circumftances, therefore, any humble attempt, however inadequate, towards removing fuch obftacles, may plead at leaft for an alleviation of cenfure with regard to the execution.

The following odes, now offered with the greateft diffidence, where by no means originally intended for the public eye: they formed, about two years ago*, part of the editor's exercifes in the courfe of his endeavours to acquire the little knowledge he poffeffes of the Perfian language; when happening to fubmit them (with a view merely to the obviating of doubts) to fome gentlemen whofe character and abilities he looks up to with refpect, they were pleafed to approve of the plan, and to declare their opinion that the publication might be acceptable. Want of confidence, however, and the neceffary attention to affairs of more immediate importance, have hitherto induced him to delay it; and it now remains with the reader to determine, whether inftead of *Two*, it had not been more prudent, agreeably to Horace's advice, to have kept his piece *Nine Years*.

The proper name of the poet from whofe works they are extracted, was *Mohammed Shemseddin*, though much better known by the title of *Hafez*, which among other fignifications, implies *a man of great memory*. He was born at Shiraz, the

* In 1772. Edit.

capital

capital of Farſiſtan, the ancient Perſis, under the dy · ·· · ·
the Modhafferians, and lived at the period wl· · · · · · ··
Timur or Tamerlane defeated the Sultaun Shah Maⁿſor. He
died in the year of the Hejira 797 (about 1394 of the Chriſ-
tian æra) and was interred at Shiraz preciſely at the time
that ſultan Baber made himſelf maſter of that city; over which
ſpot Mohammed Mimai, preceptor to that prince, afterwards
built a chapel, and erected a monument to his memory. His
poems were collected after his death into one volume by Seid
Caſſem Anovar, and have been much admired in the Eaſt for
the ſublimity of ſtile, the variety of thought, the brilliancy
of ſentiment, the elegance and eaſe of expreſſion*; but above
all, on account of the myſtery which many of the Mohame-
dans have pretended to diſcover in them, being diſtinguiſhed
by ſome with the epithet of *Lissane ghaib, the language of
mystery* †.   Hafez

* The learned in Bengal were ſo fully perſuaded of the importance of this poet's
works, that Hafez was one of the firſt that came from the Calcutta preſs. So ea-
ger was the demand, or ſo ſmall the number of impreſſions, that few found their
way out of the country; and in England this edition is as ſcarce as the moſt precious MS. This edition of Hafez, in one volume folio, was printed in the begin-
ing of 1790; it contains the original Perſian text, and an introductory account of
the author. Vid. "Oriental Collections," vol. I. p. 181. and "Flowers of Perſian Literature," p. 32, note. We are happy to add, that the ſame laudable ſpi-
rit ſeems to pervade the literati of Europe, and that propoſals for publiſhing
"the whole works of Hafez, with a Latin tranſlation,"were circulated by Mr. Hill,
of Halle in Saxony, in October, 1801. The ſubſcription is to remain open till July
1, 1802; and the work is to be printed in a new Taalik type. We heartily wiſh the
undertakers ſucceſs. EDIT.

† See Note to p. 15; and "Flowers of Perſian Literature," p. 32. EDIT.

Hafez was much careffed by many princes, particularly by
the fultan Ahmed Ilekhani and Tamerlane; but it appears
that he was not ambitious of riches nor of honours, prefer-
ing a life of retirement among his friends to the more dazzling
attractions of a court life *.

The Ghazel or Eaftern Ode is a fpecies of poem, the fubject of which is in general *Love* and *Wine*, interfperfed with
moral fentiments, and reflexions on the virtues and vices of
mankind : it ought never to confift of lefs than five *beits* or
diftichs, nor exceed eighteen, according to D'Herbelot: if
the poem is lefs than five, it is then called *rabat* or quartain:
if it is more than eighteen, it then affumes the name of *kasside*
or elegy. Baron Revifky † fays, that all poems of this kind
which exceed thirteen *beits*, rank with the *kasside*, and according to Meninfki, the *ghazel* ought never to have more

* Vide an account of the life and writings of this celebrated poet in " The
Flowers of Perfian Literature," p. 27, & feqq. EDIT.

† A fmall publication of this nobleman's at Vienna, in the year 1771, intituled,
Specimen Poefeos Perficæ, has given the editor the principal affiftance in this work.
Though not calculated for the mere learner, the materials the Baron has drawn
from Sudi, Sururi, and other learned Turkifh commentators on Hafez, joined to
his own uncommon erudition and genius, make an acquifition of value to thofe
who underftand Latin fufficiently, and defire to make a progrefs in the Perfian language. It is, however, he believes, extremely fcarce, having never feen but one
copy, which was a prefent from the noble author to his equally learned and ingenious friend Mr. (afterwards Sir William) Jones‡.

‡ Although Baron Revisky's work was very fcarce in Eng'and at the time when Mr.
Richardfon wrote the above; there are, however, feveral copies now in the hands
of private gentlemen. EDIT.

than

than eleven. Every verfe in the fame *ghazel* muſt rhyme with the fame letter ; and when a poet has completed a feries of fuch poems (the rhymes of the firſt clafs being in *alif,* the fecond in *be,* and fo on through the whole alphabet,) it is then called a *divan,* and he obtains the title of *Hafez,* or, as the Arabians pronounce it, *Hafedh.* *Divan,* however, is not always confined to poems of this fpecies, the title having been frequently given to complete collections of works, written by *one author,* in *prose* as well as *verse,* and feems particularly to have been applied to fuch collections as were made after his death. Several Arabian, Perfian, and Turkiſh authors have completed *divans,* and fome have borne the title of Hafez, but Mohammed Shemſeddin feems alone to have enjoyed it, by way of eminence, unrivalled for many ages.

The *ghazel* is more irregular than the Greek or Latin ode, one verfe having often no apparent connection either with the foregoing or fubfequent couplets. *Ghazels* were often, fays Baron Revizſky, written or fpoken *extempore* at banquets, or public feſtivities, when the poet, after expreſſing his ideas in one diſtich, impatient of confinement, roved through the regions of fancy, as wine or a luxuriant imagination infpired*.

Before,

* It is a common entertainment for the great and learned men in Perfia to affemble together, with the view to an exercife of genius, in the refolving of enigmas, talifmans, or engravings on feals, and to rival one another in the facility of compofing

and.

Before, therefore, a decifive criticifm ought to be hazard-
ed on compofitions of this kind, regard fhould be had to the
genius of the eaftern nations, to local and temporary allufi-
fions, to their religion and laws, their manners and cuftoms,
their hiftories and traditions; which, if not properly underftood, muft involve the whole in obfcurity: and it muft confequently be equally improper to fet in judgement on the
ghazel, and try it by the laws of the European ode, as to de-
cide on Shakfpeare according to the mechanical fyftem of the
French drama, or to condemn a fine Gothick building, becaufe
irreconcileable with the principles of Grecian architecture.

The leading object in this fpecimen has been to render
the profe tranflation as literal as the idioms of the languages
would admit; and as the learner is often perplexed with the
compounds, and finds great difficulty in tracing the derivatives
to their refpective roots, the Editor has endeavoured to guide
him with all the perfpicuity in his power, by analyzing every

and replying to extempore verfes, in which, from practice and a natural liveli-
nefs of fancy, many of them arrive at an aftonifhing proficiency. RICHARDSON.

In Carlyle's "Specimens of Arabian Poetry," p. 22, (poetically paraphrafed
in p 67,) the reader will find three fongs by Mafhdud, Rakeek, and Rais, the three
moft celebrated improvifatori poets in Baghdad, fpoken at an entertainment given by
Abou Ify, fon of the Khalif Motawakel. Thefe fongs were extempore effufions.
Mafhdud began; as foon as he had finifhed Rakeek began, in the fame verfification,
and to the fame air; and immediately upon his finifhing Rais commenced a beautiful little dialogue in verfe, which highly delighted the company. EDIT.

word.

word. The learned may poffibly think that he has defcended to too great minutenefs, which to them may appear unimportant, and that the repeated analyfis of the fame word, occurring in different paffages of the original, was fuperfluous ; but trifles to the intelligent are ferious matters to thofe who are yet to learn, and too much affiftance and encouragement can hardly be given to thofe who wifh to acquire languages at firft view fo feemingly rugged and formidable.

With regard to the mode of pronunciation, the Editor has in general followed that of Meninfki, with fuch alterations as were evidently neceffary to exprefs the founds in Englifh, as *jæd* for *gæd* (جمد) *che* for *će* (چ) *khun* for *chun* (خون) *muzshde,* for *muj'de* (مژده) *mesht* for *mes't* (مشت) *bukshayed* for *buks'ajed* (بخشاید). The غ he has, after the manner of Meninfki, Revizky, Mr. (afterwards Sir William) Jones, and others, uniformly expreffed by *gh,* though in many inftances which practice only can make familiar, it affumes a ftrong guttural found refembling the Greek ρ or the afpiration of the Northumberland *r.* The ع has alfo a variety of modulations, of which no general rules can convey any juft idea. As all grammatical inftructions, however, can only give the learner the mere outlines of pronunciation, his ear muft after all be his principal teacher, efpecially where the fame ftandard will not univerfally prevail in the various countries where the

lan-

language is fpoken. The Perfians differ much from the Arabians in the pronunciation of the fame word, and the native of Ifpahan has a very diftinct manner from the inhabi-
tant of Hindooftan. To multiply examples would be endlefs:
the Editor has heard a gentleman, who, from his long refidence
in Perfia, has acquired a great facility in fpeaking the
language, pronounce ابادونیدن *abadouniden*, which an Indian
would pronounce *abadaniden*; کردار is by fome pronounced *gur-
dar*, by others *kirdar*; and whilft many of the great men at
the court of Dehli pronounce the و like our *w*, at Calcutta it is
generally founded *v*. The Editor therefore begs the learner
would not implicitly rely on the manner of pronouncing
which he has adopted : thofe who go to India will be able to
judge for themfelves ; to thofe who remain at home it is very
immaterial whether they pronounce with critical propriety
or not.

Had the feafon been lefs advanced, and bufinefs permitted,
the Editor intended to have enlarged this fpecimen by addi-
tions from the fame and from other authors ; but as he cannot at this particular period, without much inconvenience,
dedicate more of his time to fuch purfuits, he has defifted.---
Should this trifle, in the prefent fcarcity of better books, appear to deferve favour, it may invite to future attempts---if
not, it is already too long.

الغزل الاوّل

الا یا ایّها السّاقی آدر کاساً و ناولها
که عشق آسان نمود اوّل ولی افتاد مشکلها

ببوی نافهٔ کاخر صبا زآن طرّه بکشاید
زتاب جعد مشکینش چه خون افتاد در دلها

بمی سجّاده رنگین کن کرت پیر مغان گوید
که سالک بی خبر نبود زراه و رسم منزلها

مرا در منزل جانان چه جای عیش چون هردم
جرس فریاد میدارد که بربندید محملها

شب تاریک و بیم موج و گردابی چنین هایل
کجا دانند حال ما سبکباران ساحلها

B

همه کارم زخود کمی ببد نامی کشید آخر
نهان کی ماند آن رازی کزو سازند محفلها

حضوری گر همی خواهی ازو غایب مشو حافظ
متی ما تلق من تهوی دع الدنیا و اهملها

The First ODE of HAFEZ paraphrased.

FILL, fill the cup with sparkling wine,
Deep let me drink the juice divine,
    To soothe my tortur'd heart;
For Love, who seem'd at first so mild,
So gently look'd, so gaily smil'd,
    Here deep has plung'd his dart.

When, sweeter than the damask rose,
From Leila's locks the Zephyr blows,
    How glows my keen desire!
I chide the wanton gale's delay,
I'm jealous of his am'rous play,
    And all my soul's on fire.

To

To Love the flowing goblet drain,
With wine the facred carpet ftain,
  If your gay hoft invites ;
For he who treads the mazy round
Of mighty Love's enchanted ground,
  Knows all his laws and rites.

But longer, 'midft the young and fair,
With happy mind and eafy air,
  Can I delighted roam ?
When, hark ; the heart-alarming bell
Proclaims aloud, with difmal knell,
  Depart, thy hour is come !

The night now darkens all around,
Now howl the winds, the waves refound ;
  We part to meet no more :
Our dreadful fate how can they know,
Whofe tranquil hours unruffl'd flow
  Secure upon the fhore ?

How many tales does flander frame,
And rumour whifper 'gainft my fame ;
  With malice both combine :
Becaufe I wifh to pafs my days,
Defpifing what each fnarler fays,
  With friendfhip, love, and wine.

         But,

But, Hafez, if thou would'ſt enjoy,
Ecſtatic rapture, ſoul-felt joy,
    Bleſt as the powers above,
Snatch to thine arms the blooming maid,
Then, on her charming boſom laid,
    Abandon all for Love.

A

LITERAL TRANSLATION

WITH

HISTORICAL AND GRAMMATICAL NOTES.

الا یا ایّہا السّاقی آدر کاسا و ناولہا

کہ عشق آسان نمود اوّل ولی افتاد مشکلہا

Elā yā eiyŭh ēſsāki ĕdar kāsān wĕ nāwīlhā

Kĕ iſhk āsān nŭmūd ēwwĕl wĕlī ēftādĭ mūſhkĕlhā;

Ho! come! O cup-bearer, carry round the wine, and pre-ſent it;

For

10 11   13   12   14   15   17
For Love appeared pleafant at firft, but difficulties have

16
since arifen.

ANALYSIS.

Ela, ya, and *eiyuh* are Arabic interjections or exclamatory particles, fignifying *holloa, ho, hark ye, come,* &c.

Essaki. الل here pronounced *es* not *el,* is the Arabic article, fignifying *the;* *saky* is properly a *water-carrier,* but here means *a cup-bearer.* The *lam* in the Arabic article, is never pronounced, when the word to which it is prefixed begins with any of thofe characters, which the Arabic grammarians call, *solar letters,* viz. س ر ز ر د ث ث ت ن ل ظ ط ض ص ص ش ; but thefe letters, over which is

generally

As the proper underftanding of this Ode depends on the knowledge of many eaftern cuftoms, the perufal of the Notes will be found very neceffary.

The poet's meaning in this firft verfe feems obvious: his miftrefs had at firft appeared to encourage his hopes ; but having afterwards treated him with difdain, he flies to wine to drown reflection. Paffages fimilar to this occur frequently in the ancient Greek and Roman poets, particularly in Anacreon and Horace.

The firft and laft lines of this Ode are Arabic ; the reft Perfian. The firft line is borrowed from a poem of Yezid, the fon of Moawiyah, and feventh Khalif or fucceffor to Mohammed. He was a prince of great abilities, magnificent, brave, generous, and humane. Like many of the Arabian great men, he had a fine genius for poetry, but, being fond of beautiful women and the pleafures of the table, his compofitions are chiefly in the amorous and bacchanalian ftyle. His manners however, which had more in them of the Syrian luxury than the Arabian aufterity, difgufted many of the more rigid Mohammedans, who moreover detefted

him

generally placed the mark *Teshdid* (˝) are founded as if they were doubled, ex. gr. الساقى *essaky, a water-carrier,* &c. الشمس *esshems, the sun,* and not *elsaky* nor *elshems.* See

him for the concern he was fuppofed to have had in the flaughter of his competitor Hofein, the fon of Ali *, and grandfon of the Prophet, who with about feventy of his friends were attacked by an army of 100,000 men, and cut to pieces at a place called Kerbela by order of Obeidallah, governor of Arabia under Yezid. So far have fome of the Arabian and Perfian poets carried their antipathy to this prince in confequence of thofe prejudices, that they have even reproached Hafez in the fevereft terms for ftooping fo low as to borrow this line from him. A poet of Shiraz thus expreffes himfelf on this head : " One night I faw Hafez in a dream, and faid to him, O thou who art fo powerful in knowledge and wifdom, how couldft thou adopt as thine that verfe of Yezid's, whilft the fertility of thine own genius could have fo nobly fupplied thee ?" To which he anfwered, " Doft thou not know this maxim, That it is lawful for the faithful to rob the unbeliever ?" In allufion to this another poet upbraids him, " Heavens ! what charm, O Hafez, couldft thou difcover in that verfe of Yezid's, that thou couldft not hefitate to make it thine own ; for however lawful it may be to fpoil the infidel, it is bafe in a lion to fnatch a bone from the jaws of a dog."

* There is alfo a ftory of Akeel, that, being difpleafed with his brother Ali the Khalif, he went over to Moawiyah, who received him with great kindnefs and refpect ; but defired him to curfe Ali ; and, as he would not admit of any refufal, Akeel thus addreffed the congregation :

ایها الناس علموا ان علی ابن ابی طالب اخی و امرنی
معاویه ان العنه فلعنت الله علیه

"O people ! you know that Ali, the fon of Aboo-taleb, is my brother: now Moawiyah hath ordered me to curfe him ; therefore, may the curfe of God be upon him."
So that the curfe would either apply to Ali or to Moawiyah. Vid. Gladwin's Differtations, p. 37. EDIT.

When Moliere came forward on the Stage to make excufes to the pit for not playing the Tartuffe, he faid, " On ne veut pas qu'on. Le joue ;" by which he meant the Prefident de Parlement, who was in his box, and had given out the order for the fuppreffion of the Tartuffe, in which he was *taken off*. W.

Meninfki's

Meninſki's Gram. 4to, p. 40, and Erpenius's Arab. Gram. p. 22.

Edar, the 2d. perſon imperative of the Arab. verb *edare* of the 4th conjugation (from the root *dar* for *dur)* *to carry, turn round, push about,* &c.

Kasan. This word is pronounced *kasan* and not *kasa,* becauſe of the two oblique ſtrokes over the top of the *elif:* it is the accuſative of *kas, a cup,* properly *a cup full of wine,* and, like our word *glass,* is often uſed to expreſs *wine* itſelf[1].

We is the copulative conjunction *and.*

Nawilha. Nawil is the 2d perſon imperat. of the Arabic verb *nawil,* of the 3d conj. (from the root *nal) to give, offer, present,* &c. *ha* is the inſeparable Arab. fem. pronoun *it,* agreeing with *kasan. Wine,* in the Arabic language, and every utenſil or veſſel employed in the making or holding it, is feminine, though their terminations may be maſculine.

Ke. This particle is both the conjunction *for, since, because,* &c. and the relative pronoun *who* or *what.*

Ishk implies *love* of the moſt ardent kind[2].

---

[1] Thus by the figure of Metonymy *continens* is put for *contento,* as 'epota vini amphora.' W.

[2] عِشْق بِاللّٰه *For the love of God.* عِشْقِن is the paſſion in Horace. Od. I. 25.

'Quæ ſolet matres FURIARE equarum.' W.

Asan,

(8)

Asan, easy, convenient, pleasant.

Numud[3], 3d perf. pret. fing. of *numuden,* which has both an active and a neuter fenfe, as *to shew,* and *to appear.*

Ewwel, the Arab. ordinal number *first.*

Weli, the Arab. adverfative conjunction *but.*

Eftadi[4], 3d perfon pret. fing. of *eftaden, to fall, fall out, happen,* &c. it is pronounced *eftadi* by poetic licence, on account of the meafure.

Mushkelha, difficulties. *Mushkel* fignifies both *difficult* and *a difficulty* : *ha* marks the plural of inanimate nouns. See Jones's Gram. p. 22. Though this noun is in the plural it here agrees with the verb in the fingular[5] : an idiom borrowed from the Arabians.

---

[3] روی نمودن *to shew the face, to appear before.* W.

[4] افتادن *to fall out, to happen, to arrive;* hence, افتاده *a nightingale,* who comes at a certain feafon. Thus ΧΟΧΧΎΓΕΣ are the *grofs* or green figs of the *caprifici arboris,* becaufe they come with the cuckows, and the mango-fifh is fo called, becaufe it is in feafon with the mango-fruit. W.

[5] Thus in the Greek fyntax we have the rule, *Neutra pluralia gaudent verbo fingulari* ; and in the Latin it is elegant to fay,

Quem juvat clamor, galeæque leves ;

Hor. Od. I. 2. v. 38. and Od. III. 11. 50.

Dum favet nox et Venus.

Gratia, fama, valetudo contingat abunde. Hor. Ep. I. 4. v. 10.

The verb is not in the fingular number merely on account of the metre. W.

ببوی

بَبُويِ نافُ كاخَر صبا زآن طُرّه بكشايد

زتاب جَعد مشكينش چه خون افتاد در دلها

Bĕbūī nāfĕī kākhĕr sĕbā zān tŭrrĕ bŭkshāyēd

Zĕtābī jăʾdĭ mŭshkīnĕsh chĕ khūn ēftādĭ dĕr dŭlhā

In hopes of the perfume which at length the Zephyr shall diffuse from that forehead,

From her waving musky ringlets, how much blood will flow into *our* hearts.

The Perfian ladies are very fond of musk; their hair particularly, which is woven into tresses, and put up with fingular art, being, in general, highly perfumed with it; the poet therefore compares his mistress's locks to a bag of musk, and the Zephyr to a dealer in that precious perfume, whom he suppofes to be fo much delighted in undoing her tresses, and loading himfelf with his fragrant merchandize, that he would be flow in wafting the fweet-fcented odour to her numerous admirers, who must confequently be inflamed with fuch anxious expectation and defire, that their blood would flow back into their hearts. This high flown oriental imagery feems to allude to the following circumftance in natural hiftory: The mufk deers or goats are found in great numbers in Perfia, Tartary, India, &c. and fhed every year a bag of mufk, which, according to the naturalifts, is formed in a kind of bladder under the belly of the animal, by the blood dropping into it, when put into a more rapid circulation from fear, defire, or any other ftrong emotion. The mufk of Khoten or Tartary is in the higheft efteem, and is often mentioned by the Perfian poets.

Belui.

Bebui [6]. *Bui* is written either with or without the final
ى as are many of the Perfian fubftantives that end in two
vowels. This word generally fignifies *smell, odour, &c.*
but as it is fometimes alfo tranflated *hope*, that fenfe is
preferred here on account of the allufion, as is more fully
explained in the note. ، *be* prefixed to *bui* is the infeparable prepofition *in, with, for, &c.*

Nafei, a bag of musk. This character ' which is called
Hamza, over the final ٥ is of the fame nature with ى following other letters, both implying unity, and anfwering to
a or *one* in Englifh. See Jones's Gram. pp. 11. 18. 21.

Kakher, which at length, compounded of ʃ for ʃ, *which,*
and *akher, at length.*

Seba [7], *the Zephyr,* properly the wind, which, in Perfia,
blows from the eaft at the dawn of day; but generally ufed
by the poets to exprefs a gentle gale breathing from the abode
of a miftrefs.

---

[6] بوى *Bebui.* Tranflate with the odour of the perfume, &c. An example
fhould be produced of *bui* in the fenfe of hope, or wifh, if the obvious meaning
of the word be changed. The eaftern as well as all other writers, ufe odour for
fame, or reputation, as in the book called Shekardân, " Happy is the monarch
whofe odour (fame) for juftice is permanent :"

اسعد الملوك من بقّه، بالعدل ذكره

See alfo Wilfon's Life of James I. p. 8, and Suidas in μῦρον ἐπὶ κεφαλῆς:
but here there is no occafion for any variation in the fenfe, which means fmell or
fcent ; and we cannot be two cautious how we extend the meaning of oriental
words that have already, efpecially in the poets, a fufficient latitude. W.

[7] صبا *Seba,* is the refrefhing wind, or the breath of love, like the gale of fpring,
نسيم بهار *nefeeme behar* that gave frefhnefs to the bower of Irem. See Cafhefi,
Fable XIX. of the Anvar Soheili. W.

Zan,

Zan, from that, compounded of ز for از, *from,* and *an* the demonstrative pron. *that.*

Turre, a ringlet of hair, properly those locks which hang over the forehead.

Bukshayed, 3d person fut. of *keshaden, to open, uncover, reveal, disclose, spread abroad, diffuse, disperse,* &c. The ب prefixed is the characteristic of the future. See Jones's Gram. p. 51.

Zetali [8]. ز for از, *from:* tab has various significations, *strength, power, heat, brightness, a fever, pain,* &c. but here it means *a braided lock* or *wreathed tress of hair.*

Jādi signifies properly *curling locks,* but in this place is a substantive acting adjectively, agreeing with *tab,* and implies a resemblance of the lady's ringlet to the waving of a chain.

Mushkinesh is compounded of *mushk* and *i* a particle which the Persians make use of in forming possessive adjectives from substantives (much in the same manner as we do in English, as *hair, hairy, flesh, fleshy,* &c.) together with *n,* which gives peculiar strength to the epithet, as *mushk* musk, *mushki* musky, *mushkin* very musky [9]. اش is the pron. possessive *her.* See Jones's Gram. p. 28.

When one substantive precedes another, it is pronounced as if a short *i* was added to it: the poets however have a licence to lengthen the sound of this short *i,* as in the above

زتاب *Zetabi,* from the curls of her musky ringlets, تاب is twisting; تاب دادن is to give a twist, or entwine (ropes) together. W.

[9] The Persians say طره مشکین and طره عنبرین Tresses of musk, and ambergris. W.

example

example *tabi*; whilft after *jædi*, the next word, it is fhort.

Che, the interrogative pronoun *how much*.

Khun, the fubftantive *blood*.

Eftad, 3d perfon fing. pret. of *eftaden, to fall, drop*, &c. but here it has a future fignificatiun.

Der, the prepofition *into*.

Dilha, *hearts, souls,* &c. *ha* being the termination of in-animate plurals.

بمی سجاده رنكلين كن كرت پیر مغان كوید
7   6   5 4   3   2   1
15   14   13   12   11   10 9 8

كه سالك بیخبر نبود زراه و رسم منزلها
1   2   3   4 5   9   7

Bĕmeī sĕjjādĕ rēnguīn kūn gŭĕrĕt pīrī mŭghān gūyĕd
1   2   3   4   5   9   7

Kĕ sālĭk bĭkhĕbĕr nĕbūd zĕrāh ū rĕfmĭ mĕnzīlhā.
8 9   10   11   12 13 14   15

3   2   1   4   6

Stain the facred carpet with wine, if the mafter of the houfe

7   5

commands thee;

8   9   11   10   12   13   14

For a traveller is not ignorant of the ways and manners of

15

houfes of entertainment.

Bemei[10]. *Be* is the infeparable prepofition *with*, &c. *mei,wine*.

[10] بمی, *Bemei.* Make the carpet red with wine. In the debauches of Antony, fays Cicero, " Vino natabant pavimenta, madebant parietes." In Horace the heir dyes the coftly floor with Cæcuban, Od. II. 14. lin. penult.; and in Athenæus we have, Let the golden goblet flow upon the pavement, Ειϐείω εις εδαφος, p. 463. But inftead of pavement our Author, more profane than the heathens, fpares not the facred carpet on which the pious proftrate themfelves in the act of prayer, and turns the *jus divinum* into *jus de vino*, by making the *Arbiter bibendi* paramount to all obligations of fanctity. W.

This word is chiefly ufed by the poets: the Perfians have a number of names for *wine*, as *sherab*, *khemr*, *badé*, &c.

Sejjade

Hafez has been confidered as the fweeteft of all the Perfian Lyric poets, and has confequently had numbers of admirers and commentators *, fome of whom, zealous for his religion and virtue, have infifted, that all his poems on love and wine are allegorical allufions to heavenly and moral fubjects, (an argument which many divines and critics have held with regard to the Song of Solomon,) whilft others have rather inclined to confider them in a ftrictly literal fenfe, efpecially when the manners of the countries where thofe fcenes are laid are thrown into the fcale †.

In

* The principal commentators on the works of Hafez are in the Turkifh language, and were compofed by Feriduu and Sudi. Thefe deferve to be particularly examined, "efpecially the latter, not only on account of his eminent fuccefs in correcting the exuberances of this fanciful and extravagant mode of interpretation, but of the fingular happinefs with which he has illuftrated the ambiguous and more obfolete allufions of the poet." Vid. "Perfian Lyrics," Introd. Obferv. p. 7. The names of Shur', Seid Ali, Lamei Sururi, Shemei, occur alfo as commentators on Hafez; but Sudi excels them all as an enlightened and accurate critic. The curious enquirer will find Sururi's work complete, with a duplicate of the firft volume, amongft the Laudian OO. MSS. in the Bodleian Library, (Uri, Cat. Perf. cxxxiv.—vii.) It would not be time ill-fpent to read attentively the obfervations of Baron Revizky, in his "Specimen Poefeos Perficæ," Procem. xxix—xxxvii. and Sir W. Jones, "Poefeos Afiaticæ Commentariorum," 8vo. Lond. 1774, p. 217—236, or in the 4to edition of his Works, vol. II. p. 467—478. (vid. alfo hereafter, p. 15.) and "Effay on the Myftical Poetry of the Perfians and Hindus." printed in the "Afiatic Refearches," vol. III. p. 165, Calcutta edition, 4to, and London edition 4to and 8vo. EDIT.

† The great and learned Sir W. Jones was ftrongly inclined to the latter opinion: but we cannot withhold from our readers the obfervations of the Rev. Mr. Hindley, in his "Perfian Lyrics," p. 29, 30. Speaking of the Ghazl which begins,

میدہد صبح کل بستہ نقاب
الصبوح الصبوح یا اصحاب

"The dawn advances veiled with rofes:
Bring the morning draught, my friends, the morning draught:"

he makes the following remarks: "This little poem bears ftrong allufion to the metaphyfical theology of the *Muffelmans*. According to the *myftical vocabularies* on Hafez, by wine (mentioned in the fourth diftich of this ode periphraftically as a *ftmi g ruby*), the poet invariably means *devotion*, and, either from contemplating the beauties of nature at fun-rife, or from having been awakened from *fleep* (there explained to be *meditation on the divine perfections*), by the rays of the folar light he may here be fuppofed to be calling the religious around him to affift in adoring the great Creator. By the *breeze*, thefe interpreters fay, is meant an *illapfe of grace*; by *perfume*, the *bope of the divine favour*; by the *tavern* or banquet-houfe, a *retired oratory*; by its *keeper*, a fage *inftructor*; by *beauty*, the *perfection* of the Supreme Being; and by *wantonnefs*, *mirth*, and *ebriety*, religious ardour, and difregard of all terreftrial thoughts and objects. (Afiatic Ref. II. 62, III. 176). This *Gazel*, therefore, may be conceived

Sejjadé (from *Sejjud, adoration)* a kind of fmall carpet on which the Mohammedans kneel or proftrate themfelves at prayers. *Renguin*

In many parts of the Eaft there are baths or houfes of public entertainment, the keepers of which are generally called *Peeri mughan*, literally *Old Wife Men*. *Mugh* in the old Perfian fignified originally *a wife man*, and was particularly applied to the priefts who had the fuperintendency of the *facred fire*; but when the ancient religion of Perfia was forced to give way to that of Mohammed, *mugh* became the common name applied in derifion by the muffulmen, not only to the priefts of the *Guebres* or *worfhippers of fire*, but to thofe of all the fects which were heterodox to the Koraun, particularly to the fuperior of the Chriftian religious houfes in the Eaft; from whence fliding into ftill greater contempt, it foon fell to be the general title given to landlords of inns or houfes of promifcuous entertainment; the boys or cup-bearers being called *mugh pcchegan*, the name by which the noviciates in the monafteries had formerly been diftinguifhed [*].

The profeffion of thofe *peeri mughan*, however, was not thought difreputable; guefts of every rank, and travellers of every nation, entering freely into converfation with them. They were in general therefore men of infinuating manners, poffeffed of extenfive knowledge in the cuftoms of different countries, and fo perfectly verfed in all the arts of their profeffion, that it was confidered as an eftablifhed rule of politenefs to pay implicit obedience to their commands whilft under their roofs. Hafez therefore, in order to convey an idea that every thing ought to give way to love, and of the refpect that was neceffary to be paid to the mafter of the houfe, infi-ceived to open with the poets impatience not to lofe a moment from elevated abftrac-tion on the Deity, and with his invitation to thofe are who filled with divine love, to regale themfelves, and imbibe *wine* on the devotional fpirit, and to thofe who thirft af-ter *wifdom*, to offer their vows to Heaven, and to give themfelves up to the religious enjoyments of celeftial and angelical love. It may be here obferved, that, deeply verfed as our author appears to have been in thefe myfterious tenets, he is alfo recorded to have given public lectures on Mohammedan Theology and Jurifprudence, and even to have compofed a ﺗﻔﺴﻴﺮ or commentary on the abftrufe and doubtful paffages of the *Koraun*. Some of his fragments, or marginal notes are faid yet to be extant. It may be remarked alfo in this place, that from various paffages in his poems, he feems to have indulged a great partiality for a fecluded and monaftic life. *Revifki*, indeed, fuppofes him to have been the fenior or prefect of fome monaftery *(monafterii alicujus fenior vel praefectus)*, though he owns he can produce no pofitive proof of this *(Hoc non aufus fim fidenter afferere)*. Procem. xxi. It is not perhaps improbable that this *Gazel* may be alfo defcriptive of the *morning worfhip* of *the Perfians* in adoration of the *fun* and its *vernal* effects upon the vegetable creation. We are informed, from good authority, that the ancient *Perfians* worfhipped three times each day; moft likely, when the fun was *rifing above*, and *finking beneath* the horizon, and its *meridian*." EDIT.]

[*] See " Flowers of Perfian Literature, p. 176. ED T.

Renguin kun, tinge or *stain*, literally *coloured make, ren-guin* being an adjective derived from *reng, colour,* and *kun* the im-

nuates, that difobedience to his orders was unpardonable, fhould they even extend to one of the higheft acts of Mohammedan impiety, namely, polluting their facred carpets with wine.

For feveral reafons frequent ablutions were prefcribed to all good muffulmans by the Mohammedan law, as indifpenfibly neceffary for their earthly and future hap-pinefs ; this naturally led them to extreme cleanlinefs, but more efpecially in every thing relative to their religious ceremonies, to which they were fo fcrupuloufly at-tentive, that the richer Mohammedans, when they had occafion to travel, or even to walk out to the fields or woods, left they might pafs through any unclean place at the hour of prayer, were always attended by fervants carrying a kind of carpet called *fej-jade,* upon which they proftrated themfelves : the poorer fort, who could not afford to purchafe thefe carpets, making ufe of a cloak or fome fuch gar-ment. To ftain thefe carpets therefore, efpecially with wine, which was fo ex-prefsly forbid by their prophet, muft have been generally confidered as a moft daring circumftance of profanation.

Thofe, however, who view the writings of our poet in a myftical light, fuppofe that by this diftich he means only to inculcate that the decrees of Heaven, however repugnant they may appear to our ideas of right and wrong, ought to be unrepin-ingly fubmitted to. A Turkifh commentator named Ahmed Feridoun has made a continued allegory of the terms of Love and Wine, as expreffing the tranfports of a foul devoutly attached to heaven ; and what indeed feems to give fome weight to fuch an opinion, is the exemplary life and felf-denial of this poet, who, when tempted (according to D'Herbelot) with the higheft offers from the fultan Ahmed Ilekhani to engage in his fervice, preferred his retirement to all the allurements of a fplendid court.

But in whatever fenfe thefe poems may be received by the various commentators, whether myftical or literal, it is not very important to enlarge upon the fubject in a publication, which is intended chiefly for thofe who wifh rather to ftudy the language than to inveftigate the principles of our author. The learned, however, who wifh to fee this fubject judicioufly handled, are referred to a work juft pub-lifhed, which difplays a moft wonderful univerfality of genius*. The elegant au-thor,

* Poefeos Afiaticæ Commentarii, by William Jones, Efq. Fellow of the Royal Societies of London and Copenhagen, p. 217. Cap. IX. *De Arcana Poematum Sig-nificatione.* Publifhed by Mr. Cadell in the Strand, 1774.
[This Commentary, which is written in the Latin language, is no lefs diftinguifh-ed, (fay, the author of the remarks on Sir W. Jones's Works, in the Afiatic Annual

imperative of *kerden, to do* or *make,* formed from the old infinitive *keniden,* now feldom ufed. See Jones's Gram. p. 57.

Gueret, compounded of the conjunction *guer, if,* and the

thor, on this fubject, conjectures that the eaftern poets who indulged their fancy in loofe immodeft compofitions, endeavoured to throw a veil of myftery over them, that, by impofing on the credulity of the more auftere and religious of their fellow citizens, they might more freely enjoy their pleafures without cenfure. He adds a moft curious anecdote with regard to the funeral of Hafez: On the death of this poet, fome of the chief men of Shiraz having objected to his being buried on account of the indecency of his poems, a violent conteft arofe between his friends and the oppofers of the funeral rites ; when they agreed at length, by way appeal to Heaven, to open the author's works, and to be determined by the firft verfe that fhould occur, which happened to be the following :

قدم دریغ مدار از جنازه حافظ

اکرچه غرق گناهست میرود بهشت

Kĕdēm dērīgh mĕdār āz jĕnāzĕi Hāfēz
Eguĕrchĕ ghĕrk gŭnāhĭft nīrŭd bēbĕhĕfht.

Oh ! turn not your fteps from the obfequies of Hafez,
For tho' immerfed in fin, he will enter into heaven.

The priefts hefitated no longer, and Hafez was interred at a place called Mofella, whofe bowers he had fo often celebrated [*].

Regifter,) for various and extenfive learning, than for pure tafte, and correct and elegant compofition. Our only material objection to this treatife is, the language in which it is written. Surely the Englifh tongue is fufficiently copious to exprefs our ideas on any fubject whatever. Why then render a work of this nature repulfive to men of the world, by writing in a language in which, it is well known, they are not converfant? It has indeed been faid, in defence of the practice of writing on learned fubjects in the Latin, that, as it is a general language, it introduces a performance at once into the great common-wealth of letters. But as the French language is univerfally known throughout Europe, and as moft Englifh works of Importance have, for upwards of twenty years back, been tranflated into that tongue, we confefs we can difcover no poffible utility in compofing interefting works in Latin, efpecially on Oriental fubjects, which it fhould be our firft endeavour to clothe in an agreeable and familiar attire. The Editor has had frequent converfations on this fubject, with different gentlemen well verfed in Oriental literature, who have regularly decided in favour of an Englifh tranflation of this very ufeful performance ; in confequence of which he has undertaken to prefent it to the world in an Englifh drefs. The tranflation is in a ftate of forwardnefs. EDIT.]

[*] See an account of the tomb of Hafez, and his epitaph at length, in the Flowers of Perfian Literature, p. 63, 64. EDIT.

perfonal pron. ﻮ. . The perfonal as well as the poffeffive pronouns may be joined to any word in the fentence according to the pleafure of the poet. Jones's Gram. p. 28, 29.

Peer*, which is pronounced *peeri* on account of the following fubftantive, fignifies *old : mughan* has various meanings, as more fully explained in the note.

Guyed, the 3d perfon pref. fing. of *guften,, to speak,* from the obfolete infinitive *guiden.*

Ke, the conjunction *for.*

Salek, (an Arabic participle) *going, walking, a traveller.*

Bikheber, compounded of *bi, without,* and *kheber, knowledge,* &c.

Nelud, is not. *Bud,* the 3d perf. fing. aorift of *buden, to be,* with the negative prefixed.

Zerah. ﺯ for ﺯﺍ, *of,* and *rah, way, road, custom,* &c.

U; and. This conjunction is pronounced *u* or *ou* when it connects to nouns, &c. forming parts of the fame fentence, and *we* or *ve* when joining different fentences.

Resm, manner, &c. pronounced *resmi* on account of the following noun.

Menzil fignifies *an inn* or *house of entertainment, a day's journey, a stage* or *halting place,* where travellers in the Eaft pitch their tents, &c. *ha* marks the plural.

---

* Vid. Mr. Wefton's Specimen of the Conformity of Languages, p. 36, 37. EDIT.

9   ●   7   6   5   4   3   2   1

مرا در منزل جانان چه جاي عيش چون هردم

14   13   12   11   10

جرس فرياد ميدارد كه بربنديد محملها

1   2   3   4   5   6   7   8   9
Mĕrā dĕr mĕnzĭlĭ jānān chĕ jāi ᵃĕiſhĭ chŭn hĕrdĕm

10   11   12   13   14
Jĕrĕs fĕryādĭ mĭdārĕd kĕ bĕrbĕndĭdĭ mĕhmĕlhā.

1   5   6   7   2   3
For me what room *is there* for pleaſure in the bowers [11] of

4   8   9
beauty, when every moment

10   11—12   13   14
The bell proclaims, " Bind on *your* burdens [12].

[11] در منزل What place is there for me *in the houſe* of pleaſure.
Horace tells Venus where the houſe of revelling is ;

        Abi . . . . .
      Tempeſtivius in domo
        Pauli, purpureis ales oloribus
      Commiſſabere Maximi.   Od. l. iv. 1.

The moral of Hafez is beautiful ; what have I to do with enjoyment, when the
bell rings in my ears,

     " Luſiſti ſatis, ediſti ſatis, atque bibiſti,
     Tempus abire tibi eſt."   Hor. Epiſt. II. ℨ. 214.

It is time for you to ſet out upon journey to eternity. The travellers in the Eaſt
are waked in the the morning by a bell, to let them know that the Caravan is going to depart. The Arabs call a perſon who overſleeps himſelf, and is not ready
to go with his fellow travellers, جثامه *jeſſameh.*   W.

[12] بربنديد Bind on (your burdens). خرج in Arabic means a double
wallet with a diviſion in the middle, ſo as to hang or be bound on each ſide of
the back of a beaſt of burden. W.

Mera

Mera (the oblique cafe of *mun, I) to* or *for me.*

Der, the prepofition *in.*

Menzili. This word here means *an abode, habitation.*

Janan, souls, but often ufed to exprefs *beautiful women.*

Che, the interrogative pron. *what.*

Jai, a place : fome copies have *emín, security,* inftead of *jai.*

Aish, delight, mirth, pleasures of the table, &c.

Chun, an adverb, *when.*

Herdem, every moment, compounded of *her, every,* and *dem,* which has many fignifications, but here means *time.*

The poet in the laft verfe having determined that Love ought to be purfued at all events, feems now fuddenly to recollect himfelf, by reflecting on his age and the tranfitorinefs of human happinefs : What has a man bending under age to do in the dwellings of beauty ? What enjoyment can I hope for in the circles of the young and fair, when Fate gives the fignal for departure ? The figure here made ufe of, in regard to the proclamation by bell, *To bind on the burdens,* alludes to the cuftom of travelling, for fafety, in Arabia, Perfia, and other eaftern countries, in caravans, for the accommodation of which the kings and great men of former times erected fpacious public buildings, called caravanferas, where the travellers retired in the evenings ; and in the mornings, in order that none of them might be left behind, a bell was rung to fummon them to load their camels and refume their journey in a body*. The word *feriad,* which literally fignifies a *vociferation,* has a reference to the mode which prevailed, before bells were introduced into thofe countries, of announcing the hour of departure by the voice of a public cryer ; a cuftom fimiliar to which ftill prevails in Turkey, where they ufe no bells, the people being called to prayers by cryers from the tops of the minarets or fteeples belonging to their mofques. This averfion to bells, according to Gentius in his notes on the Guliftan, arifes from the rooted hatred which the Turks entertain of every circumftance and ceremony peculiar to the Chriftian mode of worfhip.

* See " A Specimen of the Conformity of the European Languages, particularly the Englifh, with the Oriental Languages, efpecially the Perfian," by the Rev. Stephen Wefton, B. D. F. R. S. S. A. p. 22. EDIT.

Jeres, a kind of small bell.

Feriad, properly *an exclamation,* imploring help.

Midared, 3d. perf. fing. pref. of *dashten, to have* or *hold.*

Ke, the conjunction *that.*

Berbendid, the particle *ber,* prefixed to *bendid* has here no precife meaning, though it gives fomething of an additional force to the expreffion. *Bendid* is the 2d perfon plur. imperative of *listen, to bind.*

Mehmilha, burdens, ha being the termination of inanimate plurals.

شب تاریک و بیم موج و گردابی چنین هایل
رستگا دانند حال ما سبکباران ساحلها

Shĕbī tārīk ŭ bīmī mūje ŭ guīrdābī chĕnĭn hāīl

Kŭjā dānĭndĭ hālĭ mā sĕbŭkbārānĭ sāhīlhā.

The darknefs of the night and the fear of the waves and whirlpool *are* fo dreadful,

How can they know our fituation, the bearers of light burdens on the fhore?

Sheb,

Sheb[13], *night,* pronounce *shebi,* on account of the following noun.

Tarik, properly an adjective, *dark, cloudy;* though often ufed fubftantively, *darkness, obscurity.*

Bim, fear, danger : pronounced *bimi,* being the firft of two fubftantives.

Muje, a wave; an Arabic fingular, here ufed plurally.

Guirdabi, a whirlpool, abyss, gulf, precipice.

Chenin, compounded of چن for چون *like,* and ین for این *this.*

Hail, dreadful, horrible, terrible.

Kuja, how, in what manner.

Danend, the 3d perfon plural of the aorift of *danisten, to know.*

Hal, condition, state, disposition, mode, thing: alfo *time present:* pronounce *hali,* on account of the following pronoun.

Ma, the poffeffive pronoun *our.*

Sebukbaran[14], compounded of *sebuk, light,* and *bar, a burden: an* and not *ha* is here ufed in forming the plural of *bar,* becaufe it refers to human beings. See Jones's Gram. p. 22.

Sahil, a shore, coast, bank : ha marks the inanimate plural.

---

[13] شب *Sheb* is the night, and a black cat, whofe eyes fhine in the dark. W.

[14] سبکباران of light weights. How can they, whofe burden is light, and at their eafe on fhore, judge of my fituation, overwhelmed with the terrors of the perturbed ocean, at fea.   W.

A

$$\overset{8}{\text{بمه}} \quad \overset{7}{\text{كارم}} \quad \overset{6}{\text{زخود}} \quad \overset{5}{\text{كامي}} \quad \overset{4}{\text{ببد}} \quad \overset{3\ 2}{\text{نامي}} \quad \overset{1}{\text{كشيد اخر}}$$

$$\overset{16}{\text{نهان}} \quad \overset{15}{\text{كي}} \quad \overset{14}{\text{ماند}} \quad \overset{13}{\text{ان}} \quad \overset{12}{\text{رازي}} \quad \overset{11}{\text{كزو}} \quad \overset{10}{\text{سازند}} \quad \overset{9}{\text{محفلها}}$$

Hĕmĕ̄ kārĕm zĕkhŭd kāmĭ bĕbĕd nāmĭ kĕshŭd ākhĕr

Nĭhān keī māngd ān rāzĭ kĕzō sāzĕndĭ mĕhfĭlhā .

All my voluntary actions have tended finally *to procure me*
a bad name ;

For how can that secret remain concealed, of which they make
converfation ?

Heme, all, every one.

The poet here feems to imply, that it is equally difficult for thofe who have never felt the paffion of love to conceive the tormenting fenfations arifing from the jealoufy of rivalfhip and the apprehenfions of perpetual feparation, as for thofe who pafs their days calmly on fhore to form an idea of the dreadful dangers of the fea.

According to Sudi, a Turkifh commentator on our poet, it appears to have been a tafk of no finall difficulty to gain the good graces of a lady in thofe eaftern coun- tries ; as a lover was not only under the neceffity of paying her the higheft marks of honour and regard, but alfo to court her relations, domeftics, and even her favourite animals, agreeably to the eaftern proverb, *He who honours the mafter throws a bone to his dog.* When not fufficiently attentive therefore to thofe various marks of refpect, the friends of the fair-one were fometimes very liberal in their cenfure. Hafez, it may be prefumed, had been remifs in thefe attentions, and they had not fpared their reproaches : he is not only vexed therefore with their obloquy, but complains that all his motions were fo minutely watched, mere- ly becaufe he followed his own inclinations, and did not beftow his time and at- tention in flattering and dangling after his miftrefs's connexions, that his actions became the principal topic of converfation in their public affemblies.

Karem,

Karem, my actions; kar, a action, with the poſſeſſive pronoun affixed.

Zekhud khami, compounded of *j from, khud, one's own,* and *kam, inclination, will, desire,* &c. The final ﮔ here forms an abſtract noun, implying *a man who follows his own inclination.*

Bed nam, a bad name. ﹔ prefixed is the inſeparable prepoſition : the final ﮔ is the particle of unity.

Keshid, 3d perſ. pret. of *keshiden, to turn, verge, tend, extend,* &c.

Akher, at length, finally, the latter, last, or *succeeding part,* &c.

Nihan, concealed, hid, secret, &c. contracted from *pinhan.*

Kei, the adverb *how :* it ſignifies alſo ſometimes *a king,* as *Kei Cosrou, king Cyrus.*

Maned, 3d perſon ſing. of the aoriſt of *manden, to remain.*

An, the demonſtrative pron. *that.*

Razi[15]*, a secret, mystery.*

Kezo, contracted from ﺍﻭ ﺯﺍ ﻙ *of which.*

Sazend, 3d perſon ſing. pref. of *sakhten, to make,* pronounced *sazendi* by poetic licence.

Mehfilha, conversations, congregations, assemblies.

---

[15] ﺭﺍﺯﻯ *razi* is a ſecret or myſtery. It is alſo a plaiſterer, becauſe his art was a ſecret to every body, but himſelf, ſince arts in the eaſt were confined to families and deſcended from father to ſon with impenetrable myſtery. Builders and Maſons ſtill pretend to ſecrets which none but the initiated may be acquainted with. W.

حضوری

$$^{7}\quad ^{6}\quad ^{5}\quad ^{4}\quad ^{3}\quad ^{2}\quad ^{1}$$

حضوری گر همی خواهی ازو غایب مشو حافظ

$$^{17}\ ^{16}\ ^{15}\quad ^{14}\quad ^{13}\quad ^{12}\quad ^{11}\quad ^{10}\quad ^{9}\quad ^{8}$$

متي ما تلق من تهوي دع الدّنيا و اهملها

$$^{1}\quad ^{2}\quad ^{3}\qquad ^{4}\quad ^{5}\quad ^{6}\qquad ^{7}$$

Hŭzūrī gŭĕr hĕmī khāhī ĕzū ghaīb mĕshū Hāfĕz

$$^{8}\quad ^{9}\ ^{10}\quad ^{11}\quad ^{12}\qquad ^{13}\quad ^{14}\quad ^{15}\ ^{16}\ ^{17}$$

* *Mĕttā mā tĕlkĕ mĕn tĕhwā dæĕd-dūnyā wĕ ĕhmīlhā.*

$$^{2}\qquad ^{3}\qquad ^{1}\qquad ^{4,5,6,}\qquad\qquad ^{7}$$

If thou defireſt tranquillity, neglect not this *advice*, O Hafez,

$$^{8}\qquad ^{9-10}\quad ^{11}\qquad ^{12}\qquad ^{13}$$

When thou ſhalt poſſeſs her thou loveſt, bid adieu to the

$$^{14}\quad ^{15}\quad ^{16}\qquad ^{17}$$

world, and abandon it.

Huzuri is properly *presence* or *remaining in a place*, in oppoſition to *absence* or *motion*; and hence metaphorically

---

* This word is pronounced *metta*, and not *metti*, though written with ى. The characters ا و ى are confidered by the Arabians as confonants, their vowels being expreſſed by the points *Fatha* (a or e), *Kefra*, (e or i), and *Damma* (o or u); fo that if *Fatha* is placed over ى or و they are founded a, if *Kefra* is written under و or ا, they are pronounced i or e, and when *Damma* appears over ى or ا they have the found of o or u. As theſe vowel points are rarely uſed in Perſian manufcripts, excepting in Arabic quotations, they are more an objeé of curiofity than of importance to the Perfian ſtudent: if, however, after he has made fume progreſs in the Perſian language, he will pay fome attention to the Arabic grammar, he will foon be convinced that his time is by no means mifemployed.

[See Sir W. Jones's Grammar, p. 24, where the Perfian ſtudent is advifed to pay attention to the Arabic language, which he will find greatly to his advantage. EDIT.]

implies

implies *tranquillity, rest,* &c. The ‬ annexed is the indefinite particle.

There is a peculiarity in the Perfian Ghazel or Ode, with regard to the laft verfe, which they call *Shahi-beit, (King's diftich)*, where the poet always addreffes himfelf by name, and generally in terms of the higheft felf-flattery, to which, however, cuftom has given fuch fanction, that it does not carry along with it the moft diftant imputation of vanity or arrogance, but is confidered as a tribute of juftice due to his mufe.

The laft line, as before obferved, is Arabic. *Dunia,* an Arabic word for world, is ufed alfo indifcriminately by the Perfians and Turks. It is derived, according to fome eaftern critics, from *dena* or *deni, vile, defpicable,* &c, whilft others deduce it from *doun, proximity,* this world being nearer to us than any other. This word is often figuratively ufed to exprefs the tranfitorinefs of life and every worldly enjoyment. With regard to the creation and duration of the world the Mohammedans have various opinions, fome comprehending the creation within fix days, agreeably to the Chriftian and Jewifh fyftem, whilft others extend it to 6000 years, on the authority of a paffage in the Pfalms of David, which fays, that a day of the Lord Jehovah is equal to a thoufand of our years. Avicenna and other Arabian philofophers, affert the eternity of the world; and Thabari in his Univerfal Hiftory relates a curious tradition on this fubject, which Vaheb ben Manbeh reported he had from Mohammed, That God at the creation had built a city 12,000 parafangs in circumference, adorned with 12,000 porticoes, under which were the fame number of magazines full of muftard feed, deftined for the fupport of one bird, at an allowance of one grain a day; and that the deftruction of the world, and the general refurrection was fixed at the period when the whole fhould be confumed. Thabari was highly efteemed both as a writer and a man: his Univerfal Hiftory in Arabic commences at the creation and comes down to the year 300 of the Mohammedan hegira, correfponding nearly to the year 900 of the Chriftian æra. It was tranflated into Perfian by Abou Ali Mohammed, vizier to the fultan Abou Saleh Manfour, of the dynafty of the Samnides, who has enriched it with many curious hiftorical facts and obfervations, and rendered it ftill more valuable than the original *.

* Concerning this curious hiftorical work, fee the " Flowers of Perfian Literature," p. 68, where feveral particulars relative to its hiftory are enumerated. In p. 135 of which work is given an extract from the Tareekh Tabari, containing an account of the Manner of Cobad's Death. Cobad was the father of the celebrated Nufhirvan, and died about A. D. 520. EDIT.

E   *Guer,*

Guer, the conjunction *if.*

Hemi or *mi,* is the characteristic of the prefent, though it is often placed before other tenfes.

Khahi, 2d perfon fing. prefent of *Khasten, to desire, will,* &c.

Ezo, compounded of ز‎ا *from* and و‎ *this.*

Ghaib, absent, hidden, invisible.

Meshu, 2d perfon imperat. of *shuden, to be,* with the negative particle prefixed. *Exo ghaib meshu* literally fignifies *be not absent from this,* or *neglect it not.*

Hafez, the name of the poet : the vocative particle, (which in Perfian is ای‎ or ا‎, and in Arabic يٰ‎) is here omitted on account of the meafure.

Metta, when: this Arabic particle is both conditional and interrogatory ; here it is conditional : it fignifies alfo *that, in order to,* &c.

Ma is here redundant, having apparently no precife meaning. •

Telk, 2d perfon fut. of the Arabic verb لَقِيَ‎, implying *meeting one another:* hence figuratively *to arrive at, acquire, possess,* &c.

Min, that which, the Arabic relative pron. indeclinable, chiefly ufed with rational nouns.

Tehwa, 2d perfon pref. of the verb هَوِيَ‎ *to love, desire,* &c. The prefent and future in Arabic are written in the fame manner : in Perfian alfo thefe two tenfes are often interchangeably ufed, the one for the other, and fometimes de-

note

note a continuation of action. This word is pronounced *tehwa,* and not *tehwi,* for the reafons affigned in the note on the word *metta.*

Da-ed-dunia[16]*, throw away the world : dæ* is the imperat. of ورع *to throw away,* [in which fenfe no other tenfe of this verb is ufed] *ed-dunia, the world :* the ل in the Arabic article is not founded here, but coalefces with the following letter : *See observation on the first verse.*

Ehmil, the 2d perfon imper. of the Arabic verb اهمل (of the 4th conjugation) *to neglect, abandon,* &c. *Ha* is the infeparable Arabic pronoun *it.*

☞ The meafure of this ode is called *behr bezija,* and confifts of Iambic feet and Spondees alternately, or of one fhort and three long fyllables : the paufes in reading are pointed out by little oblique ftrokes under the lines in the European character of each verfe.

[16] ورع الدنيا *da ed-dunia* give up the world. The Arabs fay *dunia wu din,* the world and the faith, or God and Mammon, contrafting the worft thing with the beft. The Perfians fay of a man that is dead, دنيا نقل كرد است *Dunia neckl kurd uft,* He has made a tranflation from the world. Vid. fupra, p. 25. W.

ول

رونق عهد شبابست دگر بستانرا
میرسد مژدهٔ گل بلبل خوش الحانرا

ای صبا گر با جوانان چمن باز رسی
خدمت ما برسان سرو گل و ریحانرا

گر چنین جلوه کند مغبچهٔ باده فروش
خاکروب در میخانه کنم مژگانرا

ترسم این قوم که بر درد کشان میخندند
در سر کار خرابات کنند ایمانرا

برو از خانهٔ گردون بدر و نان مطلب
کین سیاه کاسه در آخر بکشد مهمانرا

هر که را خوابگاه آخر بدو مشتی خاکست
گو چه حاجت که بر افلاک کشی ایوانرا

ماه کنعانی من مسند مصر آن تو شد
گاه آنست که بدرود کنی زندانرا

دَر سنسر زلفت ندانم که چه سَودا داري

کازبرهم زدهٔ کيسوي مشک افشانرا

اي که بر من مکشي از عنبر سارا چوکان

مضطرب حال مکردان من سنم کردانرا

حافظا مي خور و رندي کن و خوش باش دلي

دام تزوير مکن چون دکران قرانرا

———

PARAPHRASE:

WITH fullen pace ftern winter leaves the plain,
  And blooming fpring trips gaily o'er the meads,
Sweet Philomel now fwells her plaintive ftrain,
  And her lov'd rofe his blufhing beauties fpreads.

O Zephyr, whilft you waft your gentle gale,
  Fraught with the fragrance of Arabia's groves,
Breathe my foft wifhes through yon blooming vale,
  Tell charming Leila how her poet loves!

O! for one heavenly glance from that dear maid,
  How would my raptur'd heart with joy rebound;

Down

Down to her feet I'd lowly bend my head,
  And with my eyebrows fweep the hallow'd ground.

Could thofe ftern fools who fteal religion's mafk,
  And rail againft the fweet delights of love,
Fair Leila fee, no paradife they'd afk,
  But for her fmiles renounce the joys above.

Truft not in fortune, vain deluded charm !
  Whom wife men fhun, and only fools adore.
Oft, whilft fhe fmiles, Fate founds the dread alarm,
  Round flies her wheel ; you fink to rife to more.

Ye rich and great, why rear thofe princely domes ?
  Thofe heaven-afpiring towers why proudly raife ?
Lo ! whilft triumphant all around you blooms,
  Death's aweful angel numbers out your days.

Sweet tyrant, longer in that flinty breaft
  Lock not thy heart, my bofom is its throne ;
There let the charming flutt'rer gently reft ;
  Here feaft on joys to vulgar fouls unknown.

But ah ! what means that fiercely-rolling eye,
  Thofe pointed locks which fcent the ambient air ;
Now my fond hopes in wild diforder fly,
  Low droops my love, a prey to black defpair..

Thofe charming brows, arch'd like the heavenly bow,
  Arm not, O gentle maid, with fuch difdain ;

                                          Drive

Drive not a wretch, already funk full low,
    Hopelefs to mourn his never-ceafing pain.

But to the fair no longer be a flave;
    Drink, Hafez! revel, all your cares unbend,
And boldly fcorn the mean diffembling knave
    Who makes religion every vice defend*.

———————

٦ ٥ ٤ ٣ ٢ ١
رونق عهد شباب است دگر بستانرا

١٢ ١١ ١٠ ٩ ٨ ٧
مرسد مژده گل بلبل خوش الحانرا

  1   2   3   4   5   6
Rŭnĕki ăhdi fhĕbābĕftĭ dĭgŭĕr bŏftānrā

  7   8   9   10   11   12
Mĭrĕsĕd mŭzfhdĭhĭ gŭl bŭlbŭlĭ khŭfh ĕlhānrā.

  1   2   3   4   5   6
The beauty of the age of youth returns again to the meads,

  8   9 7   10
Joyful tidings from the rofe arrive to the nightingale of the

  11 12
fweet fongs.

Runek, beauty, grace, elegance, splendor, &c.

* See another paraphrafe of this ghaal by John Nott, Efq. in the " Flowers of
Perfian Literature," p. 156, which is, in fome places, more literal, in others,
more flowery, than Mr. Richardfon's. EDIT.

The

Ahd[17], *age, time :* this word fignifies alfo *promise, obliga-tion, mandate, compact, treaty,* &c.

Shebab, youth ; *est,* the 3d perfon pref. of *buden, to be :* it is here tranflated *returns,* as the literal tranflation would be aukward in Englifh.

Deguer, the adverb *again :* it fhould be ديگر, but the ى is omitted on account of the metre.

Bostan, this word (fignifying *a garden, meadow,* &c.) the Arabians write without و but the Perfians ufe promifcu-oufly بستان. and بوستان.*

Miresed, the 3d perfon pref, of *residen, to arrive, follow, mountain,* &c.

Muzhdeh fignifies *good news, joyful tidings.*

Gul, flowers in general, but particularly *the rose.*

Bulbul, the Persian nightingale : it differs confiderably from that of Europe †.

Khush, an adjective, *sweet, pleasant.*

---

[17] رونق عهدى *runeki ahdi,* the brightnefs, or brilliancy of the feafon of youth is again in the fields, that is, returns, and as the Roman poets fweetly fing,

    Diffugere nives, redeunt jam gramina campis,

    Aboribusque comæ.   Hor. Od. iv. vii.

    Vere magis, quia vere calor redit offibus.   Virg. Georg. iii. 272.

Runeki is fplendor : رونق السيف *runck u's'seif,* the glitter of a fword. W.

* The celebrated Sadi of Shirauz compofed a moft elegant poem, to which he prefixed the title of *Bostan ;* fome extracts from it are given in the " Flowers of Perfian Literature," p. 144, 145, 148.   EDIT.

† See a particular account of the Eaftern Bulbul in my " Dictionary of Moham-medan Law, Bengal Revenue Terms," &c. &c. p. 47.   EDIT.

Elhan,

Elhan, the plural of the Arabic word *lahn,* a song, modulation, &c.

Runek, ahd, muzehdeh, and *bulbul,* are pronounced as if they had a fhort final *i,* on account of their being followed in conftruction by other nouns; it is here equivalent to the particle *of* in forming the genitive cafe.

Ra at the end of *bostan* and *elhan* marks the oblique cafe.

The poet here means, that winter being gone, and fpring returning, the meadows and gardens refume their youthful gay appearance. The eaftern poets allude frequently to the fondnefs of the nightingale for the rofe, with which they imagine her to be defperately in love: in thofe countries they are both forerunners of the fpring, the rofe no fooner appearing than the melody of the nightingale refounds through the groves: her plaintive ftrains therefore they figure to be only her love warblings to the rofe.

See the " Flowers of Perfian Literature," p. 157, where are inferted feveral notes explanatory of various parts of this ode. EDIT.

---

8   7   6   5   4   3   2   1

اى صبا كر با جوانان چمن باز رسى

15   14   13   12   11   10   9

خدمت ما برسان سرو كل و ريحانرا

1   2   3   4   5   6   7   8

Eĭ sĕbā guêr bā jŭvānānĭ chĕmēn bāz rĕsī

9   10   11   12   13   14   15

Khĭdmĕtĭ mā bĕrĕsān sĕrŭ gūl oŭ rĭhānrā.

F   O Zephyr.

2 3   7 8 4   5   6
O Zephyr, if thou returneſt to the youths of the fields,

11 10 9   12   13 14.   15
Preſent our reſpects to the cypreſs, the roſe, and the ſweet

baſil.

Ei, the ſign of the vocative caſe.

Seba, a gentle wind, the Zephyr, properly *the east wind:*
this word ſometimes ſignifies *youth, junevile ardour,* &c.

Guer, the conjunction *if.*

Ba is properly *with,* but here it ſignifies *to.*

Juvanani chemen [18] here ſignifies the tender herbage and
flowrets which appear in the early ſpring; though it is not
improbable that under the names of the roſe, the cypreſs, and
the ſweet baſil, the poet alludes to ſome perſons for whom he
had a particular regard; ſuch figures being common with the
eaſtern poets.

Baz resi literally *thou arrivest back, baz,* ſignifying *back* or
again, and *resi* the aoriſt of *residen, to arrive.*

Khedmet *, *service, ministry, office,* &c. here it implies
compliments, respects, good wishes: it is pronounced *khedmeti*
on account of the following pronoun *ma, our.*

---

[18] جوانان چمن *Juvanani chemen* the youths of the meadows, or young graſs,
and freſh flowrets. Thus Pliny talks of the old age of the land, *ſeneca terræ,*
when it is worn out; and Chatterton, very poetically ſpeaking of the ſummer,
ſays,

" 'Twas now the pride and manhood of the year."

From جوان *Juvan* comes *Juvenis,* with a Latin termination only. W.

* خدمتکار *Khidmutgeur* is the term uſed in the Eaſt for *a footman.* EDIT.

Beresan,

Beresan, the imperative of *resaniden* (the tranſitive of *re-siden*) which ſignifies to *carry* or *bear.* The Perſians form tranſitives, or convert neuter verbs into active by inſerting *an* before the termination in *iden,* as *residen, to arrive, resaniden, to cause to arrive, carry,* &c. *tersiden, to fear, tersaniden, to frighten.* Other verbs whoſe terminations are in *ten* form their tranſitives or cauſals by adding *aniden* to the imperative, as *amukhten, to learn, amus, learn thou, amuzaniden, to cause to teach; guerikhten, to flee, gueriz, flee thou, guerizaniden, to cause to flee, to put to flight.*

Sera and *gul,* two ſubſtantives much uſed by the poets.

Rehan, in general *any odariferous herb* or *oil,* but properly *the sweet basil* [19].

Guēr chěnīn jělwē kūnēd mŭgh pĭchē bādē ferūſh

Khaktrūb dēr mēikhānē kūnēmī mezſhganrā.

If the *lovely* infidel the ſeller of wine would beſtow on me

ſuch blandiſhments,

[19] رﯾﺤﺎن *rehan* is Arabic, and means favour, compaſſion, ſweet ſmelling herb, or baſil. W.

I would

₁₁   ¹²   ⁸   ⁹
I would make the hair of my eye brows a befom for the
¹⁰
houfe of wine.

Guer, the conjunction *if.*

Chenin, comp. of *chen* for *chun, like to,* and *in, this.*

Jehve has various fignifications, *lustre, splendor,* but particularly that ravifhing appearance which a bride makes when fhe difplays all her charms to her hufband : hence metaphorically, *blandishments, caresses,* &c.

Kuned, 3d perf. aorift of *kerden, to do, make,* &c.

Mugh peche, in this place literally means *child of an infi-*

The expreffion *mugh-peche* may admit of other interpretations : the Baron Revizky tranflates it thus :

Si tales blanditias fecerit Ganymedes vini venditor
Verram pavimentum ænopolii ciliis meis *.

or, as he paraphrafes it,

Nunc mihi fiquis calicem miniftret
Lubrico afpectu petulans-ephebus,
Ebrium duro caput in popinæ
Limine ponam †.

But as the fame imagery which paffes uncenfured in Perfian, or even in Latin, would be expofed to much animadverfion in Englifh, I have given it a different turn, which both the literal meaning of the words and the general fenfe of the diftich appear to fupport with fufficient authority. The idea I have endeavoured to preferve throughout the whole tranflations.

The poet infinuates, that if his miftrefs, who here feems to be in the character of a female cup-bearer, would deign to beftow on him fome tokens of her regard, he would fweep the ground of the tavern with his eye-brows, in allufion to the higheft mark of eaftern refpect, that of proftrating themfelves with their faces bent to the earth.

* Specimen Poefeos Perficæ, p. 71. Edit.   † Ibid. p. 9. Edit.

del,

del, applied here by the poet to his miftrefs, who placed,
it may be fuppofed, too little confidence in his proteftations of
love. See Note on *mugh,* p. 14.

Bade-ferush, a seller of wine, comp. of *bade, wine,* and
ferush the contracted participle of *ferukhten, to sell.*

Khakrub, comp. of *khak, earth,* and *rub* the contracted
participle of *ruften, to sweep.*

Der, here fignifies *for.*

Mikhane, comp. of *mi* or *mei, wine,* and *khane, a house.*

Kunem, 1ft perfon aorift of *kerden, to make,* &c.

Mezshgan, properly the *eyelids* or the *hair* of the *eye-lids :*
ra marks the oblique cafe.

ترسم این قوم که بر درد کشان میخندند

در سر کار خرابات کنند ایمانرا ۲۰

Tersĕm eēn koūmī kĕ bĕr dūrdĭ kĕfhān mĭkhāndĕnd

Dĕr sĕrī kārī khĕrābātĭ kŭnēnd īmānrā.

²⁰ This line is badly tranflated by Richardfon ; after *Kunend* he fays *expence* is
underftood, [See p. 39] ; but fuch an ellipfis can never be tolerated in any language. *Facere* in Latin is ufed for *facrificare* in a peculiar fenfe, but then the
exigentia loci makes it clear what the meaning is. In this cafe, however, there
is little occafion for fuch a licence, as the words may be rendered without any violence in the following manner : " I am apprehenfive that the very men who ridicule us as drinkers to the very dregs, would with pleafure make their religion the
bufinefs of the tavern." W.

I ap-

1   2   3   4   7   5   6

I apprehend *that* thofe men who deride *us* as drinkers of wine

11   8   11   12

Would *notwithstanding* joyfully expend *their* religion for

9   10

pleafures of the tavern.

Tersem, 1ft perf. pref. of *tersiden, to fear, dread, apprehend,* &c.

Koum, people, nation, tribe, family, &c.

Durdi keshan, literally *dreg drinkers, dured,* fignifying *dregs,* and *keshan,* the plural of the contracted participle of *keshiden, to draw, drink, swallow, swill,* in allufion to thofe jolly fellows who leave nothing, but drink up even the very dregs.

Mikhandend, 3d perfon plural prefent of *khandiden, to laugh, jeer, deride,* &c.

Der ser, here tranflated *joyfully,* fignifies literally *in defire, for love,* &c. *Ser* has a number of meanings, *love, desire, head, top, extremity,* &c.

Kar, is properly *bufinefs, commerce, converfation,* &c. but here, in allufion to the tranfactions in a tavern, which are generally all mirth and jollity, it implies *pleafure.*

Kherabat, in Arabic literally means *ruins,* but by the Perfians is ufed to fignify *a tavern, bagnio,* &c.

Kunend, 3d perfon plur. aorift, of *berden to make,* &c. *expence* is underftood *.

Iman, is an Arabic verb meaning *to protect, secure, be-*

---

    * See Note 20.   Edit.

lieve,

lieve, but is generally ufed fubftantively (for *Iflam* or *din*) to fignify *faith, belief, religion: ra* marks the oblique cafe.

This diftich appears only to imply, that numberlefs hypocrites there are who, though exceedingly fevere againft thofe who live fomewhat freely, would probably, could they do it without detection, facrifice without hefitation all morality and religion for thofe pleafures which they affect fo much to defpife.

بـرو از خانهٔ کردون بدر و نان مطلب

کـیـن سیاه کاسه در آخر بکشد مهانرا

Beroŭ az khānĕï guĕrdoŭn bĕdĕr wĕ nan mĕtlĕb

Kĕen sĭyah kasĕ dĕr akhĕr bĕkĕfhĕd mĕhmanra.

Depart from the houfe of fortune, and afk not *her for*
bread,

For this wretch in the end deftroys *her* gueft [*]:

---

[*] Baron Revifki, Specimen Poefeos Perficæ, p. 73, tranflates this diftich in the following manner :

" Exi ex domo cœli, & panem noli petere,
Nam ifte hofpitium interfector ad ultimum ad venam jugulabit."

Which he paraphrafes thus :

Quid tuis cœlum precibus fatigas ?
Et brevis fperas alimenta vitæ ?
Perfidum cunctos perimit dolofæ.
Sortis alumnos."

EDIT.

Berou

Berou beder, depart, compounded of *berou* the imperat. of *reften, to go,* and *beder, to the door.*

Khanei, a house: ' fhews that it is followed by another noun in the genitive cafe.

Guerdoun, Fortune; alfo *the wheel of Fortune, the celes-tial globe, the heavens; a chariot, go-cart, &c ∗.*

Nan, the fubftantive *bread.*

Meteleb, the imperative of *telebiden, to ask,* with the ne-gative prefixed. See Jones's Gram. p. 46.

Keen, compounded of *ke, for,* and *een, this.*

Siyah kase [21], literally *black cup, a poisoner.*

Der, the prepofition *in.*

Akher, this word is ufed adjectively, fubftantively, and adverbially, as *posterior, final; the end, extremity; finally, lastly* †.

∗ The Perfians fay, کردون دون نواز و چرخ کینه ساز Fortune fmiling on the bafe, and preparing adverfity (for the deferving.) They likewife fay, کردون اقتدار powerful as heaven. EDIT.

[21] *Siyah kafe,* black cup, means adverfe fortune, from the colour, and an enemy. —Thus Horace,

" Hic niger eft hunc tu Romane caveto."

The Perfians fay alfo *Seyah bukhti* سیاه بختی black fortune. W.

† The Perfians ufe this word as a fubftantive; thus, اخر زمان *akhire zumaun* the *end* of time: as an adjective اخرکار *akhire kaur* the laft work; اخر نفس *akhire nufus* the laft breath: and as an adverb, اخرکار *akhirekaur* at length, finally. It is likewife compounded with a Perfian verb, and therefore ufed verbally; as, (active) اخرکردن *akhir kurdun* to finifh, to make an end; (paffive) اخرشدن *akhir fhuden* to be finifhed. EDIT.

Be-

Bekeshed, 3d perſon future of *keshiden, to kill, destroy :* it may here be tranſlated *destroys* or *will destroy;* the preſent and future tenſes, in Arabic and Perſian, being often interchangeably uſed one for another.

Mehman, a guest, stranger; ra is here the ſign of the accuſative caſe.

The poet here adviſes us not to place too much confidence in the ſmiles of Fortune, which, though flattering at firſt, lead often to deſtruction in the midſt of apparent proſperity.

The epithet of *ſiyah-kaſe* ſeems here to have peculiar elegance and energy, in the reſembling of Fortune to a treacherous villain, who receives his gueſts with every benevolent appearance of hoſpitality, but poiſons their cups in the midſt of their unſuſpecting feſtivity.

In the paraphraſe of this diſtich I have given Fortune her wheel, agreeably to the European mythology, though I have not ſufficient authority to infer that this ſymbol is conformable to the ideas of the Aſiatics; yet, as Meninſki, amongſt other explanations of this word, tranſlates it *Fortuna aut ejus rota,* the liberty appears allowable.

---

7 6   5   4 3   2.   1
هر کرا خوابكاه آخر بدو مشتي خاكست

14 13   12   11   10   9 8
كو چه حاجت كه بر افلاك كشي ايوانرا

1   2·   3   4   5 6   7
Kerkĕrā khābgāhĭ ākhĕr bĕdoŭ mĕſhtī khākĕſt.

8 9   10 11   12 ·13   14
Goŭ chĭ hājĕt kē bĕr ĕſlākĭ kĭſhĭ ēivānrā.

1   3·   2   7·   4   5   6
To every one the laſt dormitory is in two handfuls of earth :

Say,.

8   9   10   11   13   14
Say, what neceffity *is there,* that thou reareft a palace to the
12
heavens *.

Herkera, compounded of *her, every,* and *ke* the relative
pronoun ; *ra* here marks the dative cafe.

Khabgah[22], comp. of *khab, sleep,* and *gah, a place.* It is
fometimes written *khabja.*

Akher, last, final, &c †.

Mesht, properly *the fist,* but here means as much as the
hand can hold.

Bedou, comp. of *be, in,* and *dou, two.*

Khakest; comp. of *khak, earth, dust,* and *est* the third
perfon prefent of *buden, to be.*

Gou, the imperative or *guften, to say.*

Che, the interrogative pronoun *what.*

Hajet, occasion, necessity, want.

* Horace prefents us with a fimilar thought :

" Tu fecanda marmora
    Locas fub ipfum funus, & fepulchri
    Immemor, ftruis domos."   . Lib. II. od. 18.

" You, with thoughtlefs pride elate,
Unconfcious of impending fate,
Command the pillar'd dome to rife,
When lo ! thy tomb forgotten lies."   FRANCIS.   EDIT.

[22] *Khabgah.* Sleeping place ; κοιμητήριον in Greek, and in Englifh cœme-
tery, place of the laft fleep, locus ὕπνου πανυσ]ά]ʊ.   W.

† See Note † in p. 40.   EDIT.

Bet,

Ber, up, near to, &c.

Eflak[23], the plural of the Arabic word *filek, heaven;* which fignifies alfo *fortune, fate, an age,* &c.

Keshi, 2d perfon fing. of the aorift of *keshiden, to extend, stretch out,* &c.

Eivan[24], *an open gallery at the top of the house, a belvidere, a hall, court, palace, garden-house:* ra marks the accufative cafe.

This verfe difplays the vanity of human life: the rich man raifes mighty edifices, but in a little time death levels him with the meaneft, and a few handfuls of earth then cover him, whofe very name perhaps made half the world to tremble.

شد تو آن مصر مسند من کنعانی ماه

8 · 7 · 6 · 5 · 4 · 3 · 2 · 1

زندانرا کنی پدرود که آنست کاه

15 · 14 · 13 · 12 · 11 · 10 · 9

Māhĭ Kĕnānī mĭn mŭfnĕdĭ mĕfr ānī tŏŭ fhŭd

1 2 3 4 5 6 7 8

Gāhĭ ānĕftĭ kĕ pĕdrūdĭ kŭnī zĕndānrā.

9 10 11 12 13 14 15

[23] *Ber eflak* to the heavens. Thus Horace of a high building,

"Molem propinquam nubibus arduis."

[24] *Eivanra.* The terrace on the houfe top had a parapet to prevent accidents. See Deuteronomy xxii. v. 8. W.

O my

3   1   2   4   5 8 7   6

O my Moon of Canaan, the throne of Egypt is your own,

10 11   9   12   13   14   15

This is the time that thou fhouldft bid farewell to prifon *.

Mahi Kenaan, moon of Canaan, an epithet ufually given by eaftern writers to the patriarch Jofeph.

Min, the poffeffive pronoun *my.*

Musned, a throne, a cushion, prop, support, &c.

Mesr, properly *a great city:* many cities in tne Eaft have been diftinguifhed by this title, as Cufa, Bafra, Babylon, Cairo, &c. from which laft, as being the capital of the country, Egypt has taken the name Mefr, by which appellation it is generally known among the Perfians and Arabians.

An, and *ex an,* when preceding another pronoun, become poffeffives, as in this inftance, where *ani-tou* fignifies *your own:* this is an idiom peculiar to the Perfian language, without the knowledge of which (fays Revifki) it is impoffible to comprehend the meaning of this verfe.

Shud, 3d perfon pret. of *shuden to be,* but here it is for the prefent tenfe.

Gah, time, &c. In fome manufcripts *vakt* is fubftituted, and has nearly the fame meaning.

Anest, the demonftrative pronoun *an,* and the 3d perfon of *buden, to be.*

Pedrud berden fignifies *to take leave, bid farewell,* &c. *kuni* is the 2d perfon prefent of the aorift.

* See " The Flowers of Perfian Literature," p. 34, 35. EDIT.

Zen-

zendan, a prison, a dungeon, &c. *ra* marks the accusative cafe.

The patriarch Jofeph, figuratively ftiled *the Moon of Canaan,* has been much celebrated in the Eaft. The loves of Jofeph and Zeleikha (daughter of Pharaoh and wife of Potiphar) have given fubject for fome of the moft elegant poems in the Perfian language, particularly thofe of Jami and Nezami. He is painted as fo exceedingly beautiful, that no woman could behold him with eyes of indifference, Zeleikha herfelf being reprefented as a paragon of chaftity before fhe faw him. This paffage points to that part of his hiftory where he was promoted from a prifon to be chief ruler of the kingdom of Egypt. The fenfe however of this verfe is fomewhat obfcure, it feeming neither to be connected with thofe which precede and follow it, nor to contain any fentiment or moral leffon in itfelf: if the allufion therefore to the object of the poet's affection, as attempted in the paraphrafe, does not in fome meafure appear to convey the meaning, it is not eafy to underftand it.

---

8 7 6 5 4 3 2 1

در سر زلف ندانم که چه سودا داری

14 13 12 11 10 9

کازبرهم زده گیسوی مشک افشانرا

1 2 3 4 5 6 7 8
Dĕr sĕrī zĕlfĭ nĕdānĕm kĭ chĕ foūdā dārī.

9 10 11 12 13 14
Kāz bĭrhĕm zĕdĕĭ keifoūĭ mūfhkĭ ĕffhānrā.

4 5,6 7 8 1 2
I know not what meaning thou mayeft have in *thy* pointed
3
locks.

That

9   10————————11   '   13   14   12

That thou haft difhevelled *those* mufk-diffufing ringlets.

Der, the prepofition *in.*

Ser, any thing pointed, the extremity, end, &c.

Zelf, properly *locks flowing loose about the ears,* or *down
the back.*

Nedanem, the 1ft perfon pref. of *danisten, to know,* with
the negative prefixed.

Ke che, that which.

Suda, passion, love, desire, ambition, caprice, melancholy;
literally it may be interpreted *what* paffion *thou mayest,
have,* &c.

Dari, 2d perfon aorift of *dashten, to have.*

Kaz, for *ke az* or *ez;* literally *that from.*

Berhem, intricate, confused, &c. alfo *assembled.*

Zedei, 2d perfon fing. of the compound preterite of *ze-
den, to strike, dash, throw against,* &c.

Keisóui, locks, ringlets: this is a collective noun, and therefore though fingular has a plural fignification,

Mushk efshan, comp. of *mushk, mush,* and the contracted participle of *efshanden, to scatter, diffuse,* &c.

E*i*

The poet here draws an unfavourable omen from the difhevelled appearance of
his miftrefs's hair: in the Eaft the ladies in general are very curious in the difpofition of their locks, which are for the moft part defcriptive of the ftate of their
mind, difordered treffes always implying ftrong agitation and refentment. Difhevelled locks are in fome parts of India confidered as a certain proof of the higheft
degree

degree of madnefs. The Malays, a defperate race, who inhabit the peninfula of Malacca and many of the Indian iflands, are fometimes (generally from an over indulgence in opium) feized with a dangerous phrenzy, during which they run through the ftreets ftabbing indifcriminately with their creffes or daggers every one who is fo unhappy as to fall in their way. This is called by European travellers *running a muck.* They are however generally difpatched like mad dogs, as foon as they difcover any fymytom of their fury, one undoubted mark of which is their undoing their hair, which is commonly woven into treffes, and put up with fingular art: this circumftance being always confidered as a never-failing prelude of their rage, any man may put them to death without queftion*.

اِنّی کہ بر مہ کشی از عنبر سارا چوکان

مضطرب حال مکردان من سر کردانرا

* From later accounts, and from our better knowledge of the Malays, conveyed through the medium of thofe who have refided many years among them, we fee not the leaft reafon to brand them with the opprobrious epithets of *defperate race, malignant* and *revengeful people,* &c. That there may be *fome* fuch among them we fhall not deny ; but we fee no caufe to apply them to the nation at largé. If we look into the purlieus of the metropolis of the Brittifh empire, we fhall find a defpicable fet of mifcreants indeed ; but furely this is not to attach to the whole Englifh nation. Befides their language is foft, melodious, and fimple, infomuch as to be confidered the Italian of India beyond the Ganges. An excellent Grammar and Dictionary of Malay in one volume quarto, has been lately publifhed by Dr. James Howifon, a gentleman of profound abilities, and a member of the Afiatic Society. From the fimplicity of the Malay Tongue a perfon may become acquainted with it in a fhort fpace of time. EDIT.

1 2 3 4 5 6 7 8 9
Ei kĕ bēr mēh kĭſhĭ ēz ambĕrī ſarā chūkān

10 11 12 13 14
Mĕztĕrĕbĭ hālĭ mēkĕrdăn mĭn ſerguērdānra.

1 2 5 3 4 9
O *thou,* who beareſt on *thy* moon (forehead) an arched club

6 8 7
(eyebrow) like pure amber,

12 1 10 11 14
Render not my unhappy ſituation *more* diſtracting.

Ei, the vocative particle.

Ke, the relative pronoun *who.*

Ber, the prepoſition *on, upon,* &c.

Meh or *mah, the moon,* but here it figuratively expreſſes *a forehead, brow.*

Keshi, 2d perſon aoriſt of *keshiden, to draw, extend, bear, support,* &c.

Ez amberi-sara, of pure or *sweet-smelling amber,* it appearing to have a reference to the *smell* as well as to the *colour* of amber.

Chuᵏan, a kind of club of an arched form, uſed in a game peculiar to thoſe countries, and here metaphorically put to ſignify *an arched eyebrow.*

Meztereb, tormented, disturbed, agitated, afflicted, &c.

Haˡ, condition, situation, disposition : it alſo ſignifies *time present.*

Meķerdan,

Mekerdan, the imperative of *kerdiden, to render,* &c. with the negative prefixed.

Min, the poſſeſſive pronoun *my.*

Serguerdan, stupified, astonished, distracted, depressed, &c.   This word ſignifies alſo ſometimes, *a wanderer, vagabond,* &c.   *Ra* marks the accuſative caſe.

Amber, meztereb, and *hal,* are pronounced *amberi, mczterebi,* and *hali,* by poetic licence, on account of the meaſure.

9 8 7 6 5 4 3 2 1

مافظا مي خور و رندي كن و خوش باش ولي

15   14   13   12   11   10

دام تزوير مكن چون دكران قرانرا

1 2 3 4 5 6 7 8 9
Hafeza mei khur we rinde kun we khuſh baſh weli

10 11 12 13 14 15
Dam tezouiri mekun chun degueran koranra.

1 3 2 4 5 6 8 7 9
O Hafez, drink wine, and revel, and be cheerful, but

12 13 14 11 10 15
Make not, like others, a falſe ſnare of the Koran[26].

Hafeza : the final alif is the vocative particle.

Mei, wine, a poetic word.

[25] *Serguerdanra.* The ſign of the accuſative caſe is not put after the ſubſtantive, but the adjective, and not after the firſt, *mezterebi,* but the laſt *ſerguerdan.* W.

[26] *Koranra.* The meaning of this is, " Don't quote the Koran againſt drunkenneſs, and get drunk." W.

H   Make

Rindi kun, drink (in the imperative fenfe) compounded of *rindi, a drink* (from *rind*, which has many fignifications, as *a drunkard, debauchee, knave, a cunning fellow*, &c.) and *kun*, the imperative of *kerden, to make, do*, &c. According to Revifki, *rindi* is chiefly ufed by the Perfians to exprefs any thing forbidden by the Mohammedan law, particularly the drinking of wine.

Khush, sweet, happy, pleasant, glad, cheerful, benign, soft, tender, delicate, elegant, beautiful, mild, &c.

Bash, imperative of *buden, to be.*

Dam, a snare, trap.

Tezwir, adulteration, falsification, imposture, &c.

Mekun, the imperative of *kerden* with the negative prefixed.

Korana, the Koran, or more commonly *the Alcoran* [*], *the Mohammedan bible*, from *koran, to read.*

The tranfition in this laft verfe is extremely fudden. After imploring the compaffion of his miftrefs, after appearing to be plunged in the deepeft defpondency, he feems to banifh at once his melancholy ideas, and drowns every difagreeable fenfation in wine. Hafez's meaning in the laft line feems to imply that there were many hypocrites who abftained from wine and flighter indulgences, but did not hefitate to pervert and adulterate the fenfe of the Alcoran in vindication of crimes of a deeper tinge : whatever therefore (infinuates the poet) your inclination prompts you to do, give way to it ; but fhun hypocrify, which (to ufe the words of Sudi, a Turkifh commentator) is a greater evil than irreligion itfelf.

[*] Although this expreffion, *the Alcoran*, be very common, and has been ufed by many good authors, yet it is certainly tautological. *Al* is the Arabic article, which is prefixed to the noun, therefore there is not any neceffity for ufing both the Englifh and the Arabic article in the fame fentence. It would be more properly written *the Koran*. EDIT.

ولهٔ ايضاً

صوفی بیا که آیینه صافست جام را
تا بنگری صفای می لعل فام را

راز درون پردهٔ زرندان مست پرس
کین حال نیست زاهد عالی مقام را

عنقا شکار کس نمیشود دام باز چین
کاینجا همیشه باد بدستست دام را

در عیش نقد کوش که چون انخوار نماند
آدم بهشت روضهٔ دار السلام را

در بزم دور یکدو قدح کش وبرو
یعنی طمع مدار وصال دوام را

اي

اي دل شباب رفت و نچيدي كلي زعمر

پيرانه سر بكن هنري ننك و نام را

حافظ مريد جام ميست اي صبا برو

و زبنده بنده كي پرسان شيخ جام را

PARAPHRASE.

Hither, O Sophist, hither fly,
  Behold this joy-infpiring bowl;
Bright as a ruby to the eye,
  How muft the tafte rejoice the foul!

Love's facred myft'ries would you know,
  Learn them amidft the young, the gay,
Where mirth and wine profufely flow,
  And mind not what the grave ones fay.

He waftes his time in idle play,
  Who for the griffin fpreads his fnare:
'Tis vain---no more your nets difplay,
  You only catch the fleeting-air.

Since

Since Fortune veers with every wind,
    Enjoy the prefent happy hours :
Lo ! the great father of mankind
    Was banifh'd Eden's blifsful bowers.

Drink then, nor dread th' approach of age,
    Nor let fad cares your mirth deftroy :
For, on this tranfitory ftage,
    Think not to tafte perpetual joy.

The fpring of youth now difappears,
    Why pluck you not life's only rofe :
With virtue mark your future years,
    This earthly fcene with honour clofe.

With generous wine then fill the bowl,
    Swift, fwift to Jami, Zephyr, fly ;
Tell him that friendfhip's flow of foul,
    Whilft Hafez lives, fhall never die.

صوفي بيا كه آيينه صافست جام را

تا بنكري صفاي مى لعل فام را

Sofi

1 2 3 4 5 6 7
Sofi biyā kē ayinē sāfest jāmrā

8 9 10 11 12 13
Tā bēnēguērī sēfaū mī hālī fāmrā.

2 1 7 3 6 5 4
Approach, O Sophist, *this* cup which is a pure mirror,

8 9 10
In order that thou mayest behold *in it* the delightfulness of

12 13 11
the ruby-coloured wine.

Sofi, a religious man, a hermit, anchoret, philosopher.

Sofi is derived, according to fome opinions, from the Arabic word *fof (wool)*, and hence fignifies a man clothed in woollen garments; whilft others deduce it from the Greek word ΣΟΦΟϹ, having nearly the fame meaning, implying a religious man or philofopher, who retires from the world for the benefit of contemplation.

Sofi is applied by the Perfians and Turks, indifcriminately with the word *Dervife (poor)* to diftinguifh a religious order of Mohammedans, called by the Arabians *Fakeers* (by which name they are more generally known in India) though the *Sofis* are however by fome confidered as a fraternity who make a more fevere profeffion of a religious and contemplative life than the *Dervifes* or *Fakeers*.

Several kings of Perfia have affumed the furname of *Sofi*, the firft of whom was Ifmael, who before he afcended the throne (about the year 1500) belonged to this religious order, and was the founder of the dynafty which poffeffed the crown till the ufurpation of Nadir Shah in the year 1736 : from this circumftance many of our European hiftorians and travellers have improperly given, without diftinction, the title of *Sophy* to all the Perfian monarchs.

Hafez, whether from the natural levity of a bon vivant, who in the midft of his feftivity laughs at all who profefs more virtue and abftinence than himfelf, or whether from a conviction that thefe *Sofis* had more of pretended than real fanctity in their affumed authority, feems happy in every opportunity of fneering at their hypocrify, infinuating that if they would only behold the cup filled with wine they would foon throw off that fevere referve, which he confidered merely as a mafk to impofe upon the ignorant and the credulous.

Biya,

Biya, the imperat. of *ayiden* or *ameden, to come.* It is a general rule, that thofe Perfian verbs which begin with ا take ب after the characteristic letters of the prefent, future, and negative imperative, as *miyaid, biyaid, niyaid.*

Ayina, a mirror, is often fpelt with one *i,* as *aina.*

Safest, compounded of *saf, pure, clear, candid,* &c. and the 3d perfon pref. of *buden, to be.*

Jamra[27], the oblique cafe of *jam, a cup.*

Ta, fignifies *so that, to the end that, in order to,* &c.

Benegueri, 2d perfon future of *neguecristan, to behold.*

Sefa, fignifies properly *purity, cleanness, neatness,* but commonly implies *delight, pleasure, festivity,* &c. The final ى after ا fhews that it is followed in conftruction by another noun in the genitive cafe.

Mei, wine; this word is more generally in ufe among the poets and profe writers.

Læli famra, ruby-resembling, fam fignifying *like to, tending to, resembling :* this word is generally annexed to nouns of colour.

[27] *Biya jamra,* approach the cup, that is, this cup which, &c. When the accufatvie is definite *ra* is added. A lady arriving in India, walked in the cool of the morning into her friend's garden, and fupprifed to find no fruit on the goofeberry bufhes, which were there planted in abundance, at length difcovering a folitary one, which fhe gathered, and eat, when fhe came to breakfaft fhe told what fhe had done, and inftantly the whole company fhrieked in chorus *goofeberryra chid:* fhe has gathered THE goofeberry.—Goofeberries are very hard to raife in the Eaft, and this fingle one had been kept for Mrs. Haftings. W.—This anecdote ferves to eftablifh a rule laid down in Sir W. Jones's Perfian Grammar, p. 17. EDIT.

راز درون پرده زرندان مست پرس

کمین حال نیست زاهد علی مقام را

Rāzĭ dĕrūn pĕrdĕ zĕrēndān mĕ̆ſtĭ pūrs.

Kĕen hălĭ nĭſt zāhĭdĭ æ̆lĭ mĕkămrā.

The myſtery *of love,* *hid* behind the veil, ſearch for amidſt the intoxicated drinkers of wine.

For ſuch things belong not to religious men of eminent degree.

Raz, a mystery, secret.

Derun, within, behind : it ſignifies alſo *the inner part of any thing, the heart, soul,* &c.

Perde [28], *a veil, curtain, tapestry,* &c.

Zerendan, comp. ; *from, among,* and *rendan, jolly fellows, drinkers of wine,* ſuch particularly as are noiſy and talkative over their cups.

---

[28] *Derun perde,* behind the curtain. Curtains were uſed formerly in this country to divide rooms. See a ſtory of Cromwell and a Jew behind the curtain in the hiſtorians of that period. W.

Keen

Mest, drunk, intoxicated, &c.

Purs, imperative of *pursiden, to ask, demand, enquire.*

Keen, contracted from *he, for,* and *een, this.*

Hal, a thing, condition, state, &c. It is fingular, though here tranflated plurally.

Neest, 3d perf. pref. of *buden, to be,* with the neg. pref.

Zahed, devout, a religious man.

Æli, sublime, exalted, eminent, &c.

Mekam, station, dignity, place, degree, &c.

The meaning of this couplet feems in general to imply, that thofe who wifh to be poffeffed of fecrets will be more fuccefsful amongft the votaries of Bacchus than in the company of the filent contemplative philofopher. It appears alfo to infinuate that luxurious wanton converfation is only to be expected where draughts of wine throw off all circumfpection, and not among fuch whofe abftinence is founded upon the principles of reafon, and who never fo far lofe fight of delicacy as to deviate into converfation which might hurt the modeft ear.

عنقا شکار کس نیشود دام باز چین

کاینجا همیشه باد بدستست دامرا

Enkă fhĕkārĭ kĕsĭ nĕ/hŭd dăm băz chēen

Kā-ĭnjă hēmĭfhĕ băd bĕdĕftĕft dŭmrā 29.

بدستست دامرا *bĕdĕftĕft dawra.* The grammarians fay there is no genitive cafe in Perfian. See Sir W. Jones, p. 17. But here is one, and *damra* can be in no other cafe ; *ergo* the fyllable را is added to the genitive, as well as the dative and accufative. *Ka inja hemifhe bad bedefteft,* For here ever the wind is in the hand (دامرا *damra)* of the fnare. W.

The

1   4   2   3.   6·   5

The griffin is not the prey of any man; draw in the nets,

7   8————10   11   9·

For here nothing is caught in the fnare but wind? .

Enka, a fabulous animal.

Shekar, prey, booty, hunting,. &c.

Kes

The Perfians, Arabians, and other eaftern nations, who in all ages appear to have poffeffed a greater fire and wildnefs of fancy than the colder and more regular natives of the Weft, feem to have furnifhed the Greeks and other Europeans with the ideas of thofe monfters whofe names are familiar to us, but whofe exiftence has long been exploded, the fabulous creatures known in thefe countries by the names of *Enka, Simurgh, Ezfhda, Ouranbad, Soham,* &c. anfwering in a great meafure to the defcriptions which our poets and painters have given us of *griffins, chimeras, dragons, bafilifks, hydras,* and other dreadful creatures of the imagination. And what feems to fupport this opinion is, that the great fyftem of romance and general belief in every fpecies of fupernatural beings, which for fo many centuries kept faft hold of the paffions of mankind, dates its origin from the return of the firft crufade adventurers from the Eaft; the *fairy* doctrine, in particular, with great appearance of probability, feeming to have borrowed its name as well as its tenets from the Perfians; *Peri* (foftened by us into *Feri*) fignifying in their language *a familiar fpirit, a good genius,* or benevolent being, conftantly employed in good offices to the deferving part of mankind.

With regard to the *Enka* mentioned in this verfe, it is thus defcribed by the Arabians, *Malumul-ifm mejhulul-jifm,* i. e. *The name known, the body wanting.* Some fuppofe it to be the *phænix*; being often defcribed as the only one of the fpecies in the world; whilft others, from its fize and defcription, think it correfponds rather with the idea of the *griffin.* Meninfki, quoting a commentator on Hafez, calls this creature a fabulous bird of immenfe fize, fuppofed to be the griffin, which, according to an Arabian tradition, is faid to have reigned as queen on the mountain of Kaf, where Alexander the Great had once a conference with her. This is the fame animal named by the Perfians Simurgh, from its fuppofed enormous fize, implying that it is thirty times larger than any other bird,

With regard to the name, it feems, according to Meninfki, to be derived from the length and colour of the neck, the literal fignification of *Enka* being a dog of the greyhound fpecies, with a long taper neck, furrounded by a kind of collar of bright fhining white.

This

Kes, a man, person, any one.

Neshud, 3d perſon preſ. of *shuden, to be,* with the negative particle prefixed.

Dam, a net, snare, gin, trap.

Baz cheen, contract, draw back : comp. of *baz, again,*
and the imper. of *cheeden,* to gather, contract.

Ku-inja, comp. of *ke, for,* and *eenja, here.*

Hemishe. properly *always :* this line therefore may be
literally tranſlated, " *For in this place the wind is always in
the hand of the net.*"

Bad, the wind.

Bedestest, is in the hand, compounded of *be, in, dest, a
hand,* and the third perſon preſent of *buden, to be.*

Dam, as above, *a net,* &c. *ra* makes the oblique caſe.

This verſe at firſt view ſeems to be merely a ſatire on vain purſuits and the miſ-
application of time in ſearching after impoſſibilities. Critics, however, who often
diſcover hidden meanings which the poet himſelf probably never dreamt of, ſuppoſe
that his miſtreſs is couched under the figure of the *Enka,* and that all his endeavours
to gain her love being equally vain as ſpreading ſnares for the *griffin,* it was folly to
perſiſt.

در عیش نقد کوش که چون آبخور نماند

آدم بهشت روضه دار السلام را

Der,

¹   ²   ³   ⁴   ⁵   ⁶   ⁷   ⁸
Dĕr ǣĭſhĭ nēkd kŭſh 30 kĕ chūn ābkhŭr nĕmāuʒ

9   10   11   12   13
Adĕm bĕhĭſht rūzĕĭ dār- ĕſĕlāmrā.

1——4   3   2   5··6   7   8

Enjoy the prefent delights, fince Fortune is inconfant:

9   10   11   12——13

Adam was driven from the gardens of paradife.

Aish is properly *life,* but here means, *pleasure, delight.*

Nekd,

The Mohammedans believe that the world was inhabited before the creation of man by the *genii,* and that God having ordered them to proftrate themfelves before Adam, and acknowledge him as their Superior, the *Peris,* or *good genii* obeyed, whilft the *bad genii* or *Dives,* at the head of whom was *Eblis (the devil)* rebelled, in confequence of which they were driven from paradife, and have ever fince continued the enemies of the human race. They fay that God, when he refolved to create Adam, fent the angel Gabriel to the earth to bring feven handfuls of the different ftrata of which the terreftrial globe was compofed, againft which the earth remonftrated, under the apprehenfion that the creature for the formation of whom fhe was to furnifh materials would rebell, and draw on her the wrath of God: Gabriel moved with compaffion carried her remonftrance to heaven: Michael was then fent; and after him Aftrafel; who both returning with reports of the earth's reluctancy, the Supreme Being, difpleafed at her obftinacy, difpatched Azrael, who feized by force the feven handfuls of her mafs, and bore them to heaven: in confequence of which Azrael, who in the execution of this office had difplayed the ftern unfeelingnefs of his nature, had the charge configned to him of feparating the fouls from the bodies of this new creation, and thence received the appellation of

the

در عيش بقد كوشـ *der æifhi nekd kufh,* In life attend to the prefent (moment) *hoc agc. Nekd* means alfo *ready (money,* and پيش نقد *pifh nekd, down with the ready,* whence comes in French *pique-nique, chacun fon ecot.* Menage fays, this phrafe is not very old in French, but does not know when it came into the language, or what was its origin.   W.

Nekd, ready, prepared, time present : it fignifies alfo *ready money.*

. *Kush,* imperat. of *kushiden, to endeavour, give attention: kush der* therefore implies *endeavour at, give attention to.*

Ke appears to be an expletive.

Chun, the adverb *since.*

Abkhur [31], has many fignifications, as *a drinker, carrier,*

the *Angel of Death.* From the different colours and qualities of the earths made ufe of in the creation of man arife, fay the Mohammedans, the different colours and temperaments of his pofterity.

Eblis, they add, being full of refentment againft this new creature, affociated himfelf with the *ferpent* and the *peacock,* who, after various arts, having at length prevailed upon Adam and Eve to eat of the forbidden fruit, the glorious robes with which they had been clothed immediately dropped off, when, ftruck with fhame and furprize, they hid themfelves among fome fig-trees, where they did not long remain before they heard the aweful voice of God pronouncing their banifhment from paradife. They were all in confequence thrown headlong to the earth : Adam fell upon a mountain in the ifland of Serendib or Ceylon (now called Pico d'Adam) ; Eve at Gidda on the Red Sea ; Eblis at Miffan near Baffora ; Hindoftan received the Peacock, and Ifpahan the Serpent. Adam, after fuffering much as a punifhment for his difobedience, was at length permitted to meet Eve on Mount Arafat, from whence he conducted her to Serendib, where they paffed the remainder of their lives.

The moral of this verfe feems to recommend a chearful enjoyment of the prefent hour, without indulging too great curiofity, or giving way to melancholy, by thinking too defparingly on the time to come ; for Adam, not contented with the delights of paradife, but wifhing to pry into futurity, was fuddenly punifhed for his prefumptuous folly, and banifhed for ever from thofe manfions of blifs.

[31] اخكور *abkhur* means a water glafs, and hence, from its brittlenefs, Fortune. "Fortuna vitrea eft, tum cum fplendet frangitur." Publius Syrus. See Mr. Hole's ingenious comment on Alnafchar and Malvolio, who will be pleafed to fee the quotation from Publius Syrus. W.

holder

holder of water, &c. but here metaphorically it means *Fortune.*

Nemand, 3d perſon preſent of *manden, to remain,* with the negative prefixed.

Adem, man, in general, the firſt man *Adam.*

Behisht [32], 3d perſon pret. ſing. of *heshten* or *heliden, to expel, banish,* &c.

Ruzei ; a meadow, garden, &c.

Dar-esselam, paradise, heaven, the mansion of peace ; dar ſignifying *a house,* and *salem peace, safety,* &c. It is pronounced *dar esselam* not *dar elselam.* [See remark, p. 5.] The Arabic Article is ſometimes pronounced as if annexed to the preceding word, as ابپ البشر *abul-besher, the father of men,* i. e. *Adam.*

$$\overset{8\ \ 7}{\text{و برو}}\ \ \overset{6}{\text{كش}}\ \ \overset{5}{\text{قدح}}\ \ \overset{4}{\text{يكسو}}\ \ \overset{3}{\text{دور}}\ \ \overset{2}{\text{بزم}}\ \ \overset{1}{\text{در}}$$

$$\overset{13}{\text{دوام را}}\ \ \overset{12}{\text{وصال}}\ \ \overset{11}{\text{مدار}}\ \ \overset{10}{\text{طمع}}\ \ \overset{9}{\text{يعنى}}$$

1   2   3   4   5   6   7   8
Dĕr bĕzmĭ dūr ĭkdŭ kĕdĕh kĕſh vĕ bĕrū

9   10   11   12   13
Yænĭ tĕmæ mĕdārĭ vīsāl dŭamrā.

[32] *Behiſht ruzei,* literally as in Engliſh, expelled the meadows, or fields, with the prepoſition in the verb. W.

In

1   2   3   6   5   4 7   8

In the banquet of life, drink a cup or two, and depart,

9   11   10   13   12

That is to fay, Entertain not a wifh for perpetual enjoyment.

Der, the prepofition *in*.

Bezm, a banquet, conversation.

Dur, time, age, life of man, &c.

Ikdu, comp. of *ik, one,* and *dou, two.*

Kedeh, a larger kind of cup, a goblet.

Kedesh, the imperative of *keshiden, to draw, extract,*
but here it fignifies to drink.

Berou, imperative of *reften, to go.*

Yāni, that is to say, alfo *undoubtedly, forsooth,* &c.

Temā, wish, avarice, strong desire, &c.

Medar, imperative of *dashten, to have,* with the negative.

Wesal, enjoyment, alfo *company, conjunction,* &c.

Duamra, perpetuity, duration; literally *enjoyment of
perpetuity.*

The poet here compares the world to a banquet, and advifes the guefts to drink
a little and then depart ; which not only appears intended to inculcate temperance
in the pleafures of the table, but alfo, as perpetual delights are not to be hoped for,
that we ought to be fatisfied with a moderate portion of the comforts of life, and
enjoy them as they come, without dreading the approach of age, or repining at the
fhort duration of all earthly happinefs.

اى

$$\overset{1}{\text{اے}}\ \overset{2}{\text{دل}}\ \overset{3}{\text{شباب}}\ \overset{4}{\text{رفت}}\ \overset{5}{\text{و}}\ \overset{6}{\text{نچیدی}}\ \overset{7}{\text{گلِ}}\ \overset{8}{\text{زعمر}}$$

$$\overset{9}{\text{پیرانه}}\ \overset{10}{\text{سر}}\ \overset{11}{\text{بکن}}\ \overset{12}{\text{ہنری}}\ \overset{13}{\text{ننک}}\ \overset{14}{\text{و}}\ \overset{15}{\text{نامرا}}$$

$$\overset{1}{Ei}\ \overset{2}{dil}\ \overset{3}{shĕbāb}\ \overset{4}{rift}\ \overset{5}{vĕ}\ \overset{6}{nĕchīdĭ}\ \overset{7}{gŭlĭ}\ \overset{8}{z\breve{u}mr}$$

$$\overset{9}{Pirănĕ}\ \overset{10}{sĕr}\ \overset{11}{bĕkŭn}\ \overset{12}{hĕnrī}\ \overset{13}{nĭnk}\ \overset{14}{ŭ}\ \overset{15}{nămrā.}$$

$$\overset{1}{O}\ \overset{2}{my}\ \text{foul}\ !\ \text{youth is}\ \overset{3}{gone},\ \text{and}\ \overset{4}{thou}\ \text{didft}\ \overset{5}{not}\ \text{gather the}\ \overset{7}{\text{rofe}}$$

$$\overset{6}{\text{of life.}}$$

$$\overset{11}{\text{Employ}}\ \text{the}\ \overset{10}{\text{time of old}}\ \text{age}\ \overset{9}{is}\ \overset{13}{\text{virtue,}}\ \overset{12}{\text{probity,}}\ \overset{14}{\text{and}}\ \overset{15}{\text{honour.}}$$

Ei, the fign of the vocative.

Dil, heart, foul.

Shebab, youth; alfo *the beginning* or *recent state of any thing.*

Rift, 3d perfon pref. of *riften*, *to go.*

Nechidi, 2d perfon of *chiden*, *to gather, pluck*, &c. with the negat. prefixed.

Guli, *the rose*, the final ی here being equivalent to the definite article *the* in Englifh.

Zumr, from *life* : *ŭmr signifies* properly *an age, a long life.*

Peerane, *old age*, from *peer*, *an old man.*

Ser has a variety of fignifications ; here it means *time.*

Bekun,

Bekun, the imperative of *kerden, to make.*

Henri, virtue, science, excellency, art, &c.

Nenk, probity, virtue, honour, &c.

Nam, name, fame, honour, reputation, &c.

The poet in this verſe evidently adviſes us not to repine too much at what is paſt and cannot be recalled ; but that if the reflection on our early age ſhould recall to our recollection more of folly than of prudence, we ſhould endeavour to compenſate for our youthful negligence in gathering the roſe of life, by the exemplary conduct of our declining years.

حافظ مرید جام میست ای صبا برو

و زبنده بنده کی یرسان شیخ جام را

Hafez mĕrīd jāmĭ mĕſt eĭ sĕbă bĕrū

Vĕ zĕ bĭndĕ bĕndĕkĭ bĕrsān ſheĭkh jāmrā.

Hafez is deſirous of a cup of wine, fly, O Zephyr,

And from *his* ſervant, preſent reſpects to Sheikh Jami.

Merid, is a participle of the 4th form of Arabic verbs, and ſignifies *deſirous.*

Jam, a cup, globe, &c.

Meiſt, mei, wine, with the 3d perſon preſent of *buden, to be,* annexed.

K

Ei,

Ei seba, the vocative of *seba, a gale.*

Berou, imperative of *reften, to go.*

Zebende, compounded of *j from,* and *bende, a servant.*

Bendeki, service, servitude : here it means *compliments, respects :* it is the abſtract from *bende, a servant.*

Bersan or *beresan,* imperat. of *resaniden, to carry, bear,* &c. the tranſitive of *residen, to arrive.*

Sheikh, a doctor, a learned man, a senior, old man, &c.

Jam, there is a play words of here, *jam* ſignifying not only *a cup,* but being the name of one of our poet's friends, author of a work called *enis-essabitin,* i. e. *the Constant Friend.*

The eaſtern nations make their cups of many different metals as well as glaſs : they have great variety of ſhapes, but moſtly tending to the ſpheric, whence *jam* ſignifies alfo *the celeſtial globe :* from the brightneſs of theſe cups *jam* alſo means ſometimes *a mirror.* They have a tradition, that *Jemſhid* (the Solomon of the Perſians) and Alexander the Great had cups, which ſhewed them all things, natural and even ſupernatural : the patriarch Joſeph is ſaid to have uſed a myſterious cup when he foretold future events ; and Homer deſcribes the cup of old Neſtor, on which all nature was ſymbolically repreſented. One nation probably borrowed the idea from another, but where it originated it is difficult to determine, though the preſumption is rather in favour of the eaſtern nations, as the marvellous has in all ages prevailed more with them than among the philoſophic and reaſoning Europeans.

ADDITIONAL NOTES AND ILLUSTRATIONS.

PAGE 6.   The paffage concerning Moawiyah and Yezid may be in fome meafure illuftrated by the following anecdote of Yezid's mother:

" Maifuna was a daughter of the tribe of Calab ; a tribe according to Abulfeda, remarkable for the purity of dialect fpoken in it, and for the number of poets it had produced.   She was married, whilft very young, to the Khalif Moawiyah. But this exalted fituation by no means fuited the difpofition of Maifuna, and amidft all the pomp and fplendour of Damafcus, fhe languifhed for the fimple pleafures of her native defert.

" Thefe feelings gave birth to the following fimple ftanzas, which fhe took the greateft delight in finging, whenever fhe could find an opportunity to indulge her melancholy in private.   She was unfortunately overheard one day by Moawiyah, who was of courfe not a little offended wich fuch a difcovery of his wife's fentiments ; and, as a punifhment for her fault, he ordered her to retire from court. Maifuna immediately obeyed, and taking her infant fon Yezid with her, returned to Yeman : nor did fhe revifit Damafcus till after the death of Moawiyah, when Yezid afcended the throne."

Here follow the Arabic ftanzas which gave umbrage to Moawiyah :

للبس عبا وتقر عيني
احب الي من لبس الشفوف
وبيت تختفق الارواح فيه
احب الي من قصر منيف [33]
وبكر يتبع الاظعان صعب
احب الي من بغل رفوف
وكلب ينبح الاضياف دوني
احب الي من هر الدفوف
وخرق من بني عمي فقير
احب الي من علج عليف

[33] A literal tranflation of Maifuna's two firft couplets :
" Cloaths of coarfe cloth, roots of (genuine) nature to me (are) more lovely than their tranfparent dreffes : and a low roofed houfe, through which the breezes whifper, spervious to the whifpering breeze, pleafe me more than the lofty palace."   W.

Tнв

" THE ruffet fuit of camel's hair,
  With fpirits light and eye ferene,
Is dearer to my bofom far
  Than all the trappings of a queen.

The humble tent and murmuring breeze
  That whiftles thro' its fluttering walls,
My unafpiring fancy pleafe
  Better than towers and fplendid halls.

Th' attendant colts that bounding fly
  And frolic by the litter's fide,
Are dearer in MAISUNA's eye
  Than gorgeous mules in all their pride.

The watch dog's voice that bays whene'er
  A ftranger feeks his mafter's cot,
Sound's fweeter in MAISUNA's ear,
  Than yonder trumpet's long-drawn note.

The ruftic youth unfpoil'd by art,
  Son of my kindred, poor but free,
Will ever to MAISUNA's heart
  Be dearer, pamper'd fool, than thee."

" Moawiyah was the fifth (fed quære) Khalif in fucceffion from Mohammed, and the founder of the Ommiad dynafty. He fhewed a violent oppofition at firft to the new religion, but having profeffed himfelf a convert, he was received into great favour by the Prophet, and advanced to the higheft dignities by the fucceeding Khalifs, Abubecr, Omar, Othman, the laft of whom appointed him governor of Egypt.

Upon the murder of Othman, Moawiyah determined to revenge his death, and accordingly declared an irreconcileable enmity to the houfe of Ali, by whofe fuggeftitions he confidered the crime to have been perpetrated.

The confequence of this was a long and bloody war between the Alidies and Moawiyah, which at length terminated in favour of the latter. But though, during the conteft, Moawiyah gave innumerable proofs of his valour and abilities, he was indebted for his ultimate fuccefs more to the moderation of his competitor Haffan, the fon of Ali, than to his own conduct; for this virtuous prince having beheld with horror the effufion of fo much Moflem blood, refolved to put a ftop to it, by giv-

ing

ing up is own pretenfions to the throne : this refolution he executed in the 40th year of the Hejira, and upon his abdication, Moawiyah was acknowledged through the empire *Commander of the Faithful.*

Moawiyah difplayed as many virtues when in poffeffion of the Khalifat as he had fhewn talents in acquiring it, and after a glorious reign of nineteen years died at Damafcus univerfally regretted.

The laft public fpeech he made to his people is ftill preferved : " I am like corn that is to be reaped," faid the dying monarch. " I have governed you till we are weary of one another ; I am fuperior to all my fucceffors, as my predeceffors were fuperior to me : God defires to approach all who defire to approach him ; O God, I love to meet thee, do thou love to meet me !" Vide Carlyle's Specimen of Arabian Poetry, p. 37.

While we are fpeaking of the family of Yezid, it may not be amifs to lay before our readers an anecdote of that monarch, which is but little known to the generality of Europeans. Yezid fucceeded his father Moawiyah in the Khalifat A. H. 60 ; and in moft refpects fhewed himfelf to be of a very different difpofition from his predeceffor.

He was naturally cruel, avaricious, and debauched ; but inftead of concealing his vices from the eyes of his fubjects, he feemed to make a parade of thofe actions, which he knew no good Muffulman could look upon without horror ; he drank wine in public, he careffed his dogs, and was waited upon by his eunuchs in fight of the whole court.

Such a conduct, particularly when contrafted with the piety of the former Khaliffs, with reafon gave great fcandal to the Mohammedan world ; and accordingly we find the fhort reign of Yezid perpetually difturbed with tumults and infurrections.

This prince notwithftanding the many crimes and follies he was guilty of, inherited his mother Maifuna's tafte for poetry. Many of his compofitions upon different occafions are tranfmitted to us by Arabian hiftorians : I have felected the following one as a fpecimen both of his profligacy and wit :

امين شربة من ما كرم شربتها
غضبت علي الان طاب السكر
ساشرب فاغضب لا رضيت كلاهبا
حبيب الي قلبي عقوتك والخمر

Muft

" Must then my failings from the fhaft
    Of anger ne'er efcape ?
And doft thou ftorm becaufe I've quaff'd
    The water of the grape ?

That I can thus from wine be driv'n
    Thou furely ne'er canft think—
Another reafon thou haft giv'n
    Why I refolve to drink.

'Twas fweet the flowing cup to feize,
    'Tis fweet thy rage to fee ;
So firft I drink myfelf to pleafe,
    And next—to anger thee."   Carlyle's Specimen, p. 39.

Page 6. Some account of the folemn feftival in the month Mohurrum, the ftory of Hofein, the fon of Ali, the anecdote of an European ambaffador, the pageants and other ceremonies during the Mohurrum, the enthufiafm of the Perfians during the Mohurrum, &c. will be found illuftrative of feveral paffages in this as well as in other works, and will convey a portion of information on various particulars hitherto but imperfectly known in Europe. Although the extract be long, yet, by reafon of its utility, our readers will readily excufe us.

" The firft ten days of the month Mohurrum (being the firft of the Mohammedan year) are obferved throughout Perfia as a folemn mourning ; it is called by the natives *Dèha*, or a fpace of ten days. During this period the Perfians and all the followers of Ali, lament the death of Imaum Hoffein, the fecond fon of that prophet, who was flain in the war againft Yezid, the fon of Moawiyah, Khalif of the Muffulmans. This event happened at a place called Kerbela, which in Perfian implies *grief and misfortune*. It is fituated in Irak Arabi, the ancient Mefopotamia, between the cities of Cufa and Medina.—The particulars of the ftory are as follow :

" On the death of Khalif Ali, who was affaffinated at Cufa, Moawiyah of the houfe of Ommia, fucceeded to the Khalifat, which he had difputed with Ali during his lifetime. Moawiyah, dying fhortly after, was fucceeded by his
                                                                          eldeft

eldeft fon Yezid. In the interval *, the inhabitants of Cufa had fent a folemn
embaffy to Hoffein at Medina, requefting him to come and take poffeffion of the
government, giving affurance of their faithful fupport. Upon this affurance,
Hoffein determined to fet forwards, at the fame time taking with him the whole of
his family (excepting his youngeft daughter, who was at that time fick). He began is march to Cufa on the 8th of Zulhuj, accompanied by a confiderable body
of troops : intelligence of this being carried to the Khalif Yezid, who was then
at Damafcus, he fent orders to Obeidollah, the Governor of Cufa, to affemble an
army and to crufh the rifing rebellion, by cutting off Hoffein and his followers.
Obeidollah, in obedience to the command of his mafter, fent his deputy Ibn Saàd, with
ten thoufand men, giving him exprefs orders to intercept Hoffein in his route.—The
army in confequence began their march ; Obeidollah, remaining in the city, took care
by feizing the heads of the faction, intirely to quell the infurrection ; by which
means, the Cufians perceiving the fituation of affairs, regardlefs of the oaths and pro-
mifes they had made, treacheroufly left the unhappy prince to his fate ; for which behaviour they are curfed by the Perfians and the followers of Ali to this day. Hoffein
with his army had not advanced far, before intelligence was brought him that the
enemy had taken their ftation between him and the river Euphrates, which lay
in his intended route, by means of which he was intirely cut off from the water ;
an event of the moft diftreffing nature in the fultry climate of Mefopotamia, where,
from the violence of the heat, the weary traveller, even when fuplied with water,
can fcarcely exift.—Deprived of that neceffary article, how trying muft the fituation be ! Indeed this circumftance was the preliminary caufe of all the misfortunes which befel him :—his men, difheartened at the idea of perifhing with thirft,
forfook him in great numbers, deferting fo very faft, that in few days his force was
reduced to the inconfiderable number of feventy-two perfons, among whom, were
feveral of his own kindred, particularly his brother Abbàs Ali, his nephew Càfim
the fon of his brother Haffan, his own fon Zein al Abudeen, a youth of twelve
years of age, and his two infant children, Akbur and Afkur ; of the females,
were his daughter Sekeena, his fifter Zeinib, and his aunt Koolfom.—In this fituation, continual fkirmifhes and diftreffes thickening upon him, were finally terminated on the tenth of Mohurrum, when Ibn Saàd advancing with his whole force,
furrounded this little troop, and they were cut to pieces, after fighting moft defperately. Afkur, Hoffein's infant fon, was killed by arrows in his father's

* Anno Hejira 60.

lap ;

lap; and Hoffein himfelf, at length laid exhaufted with fatigue, and fainting under a multitude of wounds, fell. His head was immediately cut off, and the enemy's troops then rufhing into the tent began a general plunder, and took prifoners the remaining fon of Hoffein, who was fick in bed, together with the females of the family already mentioned; bereaving them at the fame time of their ornaments and jewels, and treating them in a moft infulting manner. A few days after, they were all conveyed to Damafcus, with the head of Hoffein, to be prefented to the Khalif Yezid.

The tradition goes, that at this period an ambaffador from one of the European ftates happened to refide at the Khalif's court, who on the arrival of the prifoners, was ftruck with compaffion at the miferable appearance they mnde, and afked Yezid who they were; the Khalif replied, that they were of the family of the prophet Mohammed, and that the head was the head of Hoffein the fon of Ali, whom he had caufed to be put to death for his rebellion; whereupon the ambaffador rofe up and reviled the Khalif very bitterly for thus treating the family of his own prophet. The haughty Yezid, enraged at the affront, ordered the ambaffador to go himfelf and bring him the head of Zein al Abudeen, on pain of immediate death; this however the ambaffador flatly refufed; and, as the Perfians believe, embracing the head of Hoffein, turned Muffulman; on which he was immediately put to death by the command of Yezid.

All thefe various events are reprefented by the Perfians during the firft ten days of Mohurrum. On the 27th of the preceding month of Zúlhuj, they erect the Mumbirs on the pulpits of the mofques, the infides of which are on this occafion lined with black cloth. On the 1ft of Mohurrum the Akhunds of Peifh Numazz's (or Mohammedan priefts) mount the pulpits, and begin what is denominated by the Perfians al Wakad, or a recital of the life and actions of Ali, and his fons Huffun and Hoffein; defcribing at the fame time the circumftances attending the melancholy fate of the Imaum Hoffein; the recital is made in a low folemn tone of voice, and is really affecting to hear, being written with all the pathetic elegance the Perfian language is capable of expreffing. At intervals the people ftrike their breafts with violence, weeping bitterly at the fame time, and exclaiming, "Ah Hoffein! ah Hoffein! Heif az Hoffein! Alas for Hoffein!"—Other parts of the Wakad are in verfe, which are fung in cadence to a doleful tune. Each day fome particular action of the ftory is reprefented by people felected for the purpofe of perfonating thofe concerned in it; effigies are alfo brought out and carried in proceffion through the different neighbourhoods; among thefe they have one reprefenting

the

the river Euphrates, which they call *Abi Forat*. Troops of boys and young men, some perfonating the foldiers of Ibn Saad, others thofe of Hoffein and his company, run about the ftreets, beating and fkirmifhing with each other, and each have their refpective banners and enfigns of diftinction. Another pageant reprefents the Khalif Yezid feated on a magnificent throne furrounded by guards; and by his fide is placed the European ambaffador afore-mentioned.

Among the moft affecting reprefentations is the marriage of young Cafim, the fon of Huffun, and nephew of Hoffein, with his daughter; but this was never confummated, as Cafim was killed in a fkirmifh on the banks of the Euphrates, on the 7th of Mohurrum. On this occafion a boy reprefents the bride, decorated in her wedding garments, and attended by the females of the family chanting a mournful elegy, in which is related the circumftance of her betrothed hufband being cut off by infidels—(for fuch is the term by which the Shelas fpeak of the Sunnies). The parting between her and her hufband is alfo reprefented, when on going to the field fhe takes an affectionate leave of him; and, on his quitting her, prefents him with a burial veft, which fhe puts round his neck: at this fight the people break out into moft paffionate exclamations of grief and diftrefs, and execrate the moft bitter curfes upon Yezid, and all thofe who had any concern in deftroying the family of their Imaum.

The facred pigeons, which are affirmed by the Perfians to have carried news of Hoffein's death from Kerbelai to Medina (having firft dipped their beaks in his blood as a confirmation), are alfo brought forth on this occafion. The horfes on which Hoffein and his brother Abbas are fuppofed to have rode, are fhewn to the people, painted as covered with wounds, and ftuck full of arrows.

During thefe various proceffions much injury is often fuftained, as the Perfians are all frantic even to enthufiafm, and they believe uniformly that the fouls of thofe flain during the Mohurrum will infallibly go that inftant into *Paradife*; this, added to their frenzy, which, for the time it lafts, is fuch as I never faw exceeded by any people, makes them defpife and even court death. Many there are who inflict voluntary wounds on themfelves, and fome who almoft entirely abftain from water during thefe ten days, in memory of, and as a fufferance for, what their Imaum fuffered from the want of that article; all people abftain from the bath, and even from changing their clothes during the continuance of the *Mohurrum*. On the 10th day, the coffins of thofe flain in the battle are brought forth, ftained with blood, on which fcymitars and turbans, adorned with herons' feathers, are laid:—thefe are folemnly interred, after which the priefts again mount the pulpits and read the Wakaà. The whole is concluded with curfes and imprecations on the Khalif Yezid.

L.

The

The Perſians affirm this to be a martyrdom, and throughout the whole of the recital Hoffein is diftinguifhed by the appellation of *Sheheed*, or the martyr. They add, that he alfo knew of, and voluntarily fuffered it as an expiation for the fins of all who believe in Ali, and confequently that all who lament the death of their Imaum, fhall find favour at the day of judgement: they further affert, that if Hoffein had thought proper to make ufe of the powers of his Imaumfhip, the whole world could not have hurt him, but that he chofe to fuffer a voluntary death, that his followers might reap the benefit of it in a future ftate: whence arifes the belief among tha Perfians, that at the day of judgement Fatima, the wife of Ali, and mother of the two Imaums Huffun and Hoffein, will prefent herfelf before the throne of God, with the fevered head of Hoffein in one hand, and the heart of Huffun (who was poifoned) in the other, demanding abfolution in their names for the fins of the follows of Ali; and they doubt not but God will grant their re-queft.—I had thefe particulars from a religious Perfian, and as they are not gene-rally known to Europeans, I have taken the liberty of inferting them.

The death of the Imaum Huffun (who was poifoned by Ayèfha the widow of Mo-hammed at Medina) is lamented by the followers of Ali on the 28th of the month Sefr, being the day on which he died, but it is not kept with fo great a folemnity as thofe of Mohurrum; although Huffun is mentioned during that period. Many perfons have confounded thefe together, and erroneoufly fuppofe the *Deha* of Mo-hurrum to be equally for both; I was particularly inquifitive on this head, and was affured by feveral perfons that the diftinétion between the two was very confidera-ble." See Francklin's Tour from Bengal to Perfia, p. 239, &c.

Page 17. The Arabians ufe ‏أم البنزل‏ *ummu 'l'menzili*, by which they mean a hoftefs, a landlady, or the mother of a family.

Page 18. The following extraét from " Obfervations made on a Tour from Bengal to Perfia," by William Francklin, p. 257, will defcribe the mode of tra-velling in Perfia:

" A *Cafila* is compofed of camels, horfes, and mules, the whole of which are under the direétion of a Cheharwa Dar, or Mafter. It is to him the price of a mule or camel is paid, and he ftipulates with the traveller to feed and take care of the beaft during the journey; he has under him feveral inferior fervants, who help to unload the beafts of burden, take them to water, and atten l them during forage. The Cafila, whilft on the journey, keeps as clofe as poffible, and on its arrival at the *Munzil Gah*, or place of encampment for the day, each load is depofited on a particular fpot

marked

marked out by the mafter, to which the merchant who owns the goods repairs ;
his baggage forms a crefcent ; in the centre are placed the bedding and provifions :
a rope or line made of hair is then drawn round the whole, at the diftance of about
three yards each way, which ferves to diftinguifh the feparate encampments. During the night, the beafts are all brought to their ftations, oppofite to the goods they
are to carry in the morning, and are made faft to the hair rope above mentioned.
At the hour of moving, which is generally between three and four in the morning,
they load the mules and camels. In doing this, the paffengers are awakened by
the jingling of the bells tied round the necks of the beafts, in order to prevent
their ftraggling during the march. A paffage from Hafiz may probably be not un-
acceptable to the reader in this place, as it ferves to illuftrate the cuftom above defcribed :

جرس فرياد ميدارد كه بربنديد محملها

" The bell proclaims aloud, bind *on your burdens* ?"   ODES OF HAFEZ.

When every thing is ready, the Cheharwa Dar orders thofe neareft the road to
advance, and the whole move off in regular fucceffion, in the fame order as the
preceding day."

Page 43. Add to Note [24]. The houfes in the Eaft were in ancient times, as
they are ftill generally built, in one and the fame uniform manner. The roof or
top of the houfe is always flat, covered with broad ftones, or a ftrong plafter of
terrace, and guarded on every fide with a low parapet wall. (*Deut.* xxii. 8.) The
terrace is frequented as much as any part of the houfe. On this, as the feafon fa-
vours, they walk, they eat, they fleep, they tranfact bufinefs, (1 *Sam.* ix. 25.)
they perform their devotions. (*Acts* x. 9.) The houfe is built with a court
within, into which chiefly the windows open ; thofe that open to the ftreets,
are fo obftructed with lattice work, that no one either without or within can
fee through them. Whenever therefore any thing is to be feen or heard in the ftreets,
every one immediately goes up to the houfe-top to fatisfy his curiofity. In the fame
manner, when any one had occafion to make any thing public, the readieft and
moft effectual way of doing it, was to proclaim it from the houfe-tops to the people in the ftreets. (*Matth.* x. 27.) Vid. Bp. Lowth on Ifaiah xxii. 1.

Dr. Shaw acquaints us, that " the houfes throughout the Eaft are low, having
generally a ground floor only, or one upper ftory, and flat roofed, the roof being

L 2   covered

covered with a ftrong coat of plafter of terrace. They are built round a paved court, into which the entrance from the ftreet is through a gateway or paffage-room, furnifhed with benches, and fufficiently large to be ufed for receiving vifits or tranfacting bufinefs. The ftairs which lead to the roof are never placed on the outfide of the houfe in the ftreet, but ufually in the gateway, or paffage-room to the court, fometimes at the entrance within the court. This court is now called in Arabic, *el wooft*, or the middle of the houfe; literally anfwering to $\tau o \ \mu \varepsilon \sigma o \nu$ of *St. Luke* v. 19. It is cuftomary to fix cords from the parapet walls (*Deut.* xxii. 8.) of the flat roofs acrofs this court, and upon them to expand a veil or covering as a fhelter from the heat. In this area probably our Saviour taught. The paralytic was brought on to the roof by making a way through the crowd to the ftairs in the gateway, or by the terraces of the adjoining houfes. They rolled back the veil, and let the fick man down over the parapet of the roof into the area or court of the houfe, before Jefus." Vid. Shaw's Travels, p. 277.

In the center of Shirauz is a mofque, which the Perfians call يو جد ﻣﺳ Musjidi Noo, or the new mofque; but its date is nearly coeval with the city itfelf, at leaft fince it has been inhabited by Mohammedans; it is a fquare building of a noble fize, and has apartments for prayer on each fide; in them are many infcriptions in the old Cufic character, which of themfelves denote the antiquity of the place; in the center of the fquare is a large terrace, on which the Perfians perform their devotions, both morning and evening; this terrace is capable of containing upwards of two hundred perfons, and is built of ftone raifed two feet and a half high from the ground; there are two very large cyprefs trees of an extraordinary height, which the Perfians affirm to have ftood the amazing length of fix hundred years: they are called Aafhuk Maafhuka, or the lover and his miftrefs, and are held in great veneration. The mofque has a garden adjoining to it, and places neceffary for performing ablutions. Vid. Francklin's Tour, p. 64.

Page 45. It.may not be amifs in this place to illuftrate what is faid by Mr. Richardfon relative to Jofeph, by a paffage from the Koranic furat or chapter concerning that patriarch, on a comparifon of which, with the Biblical account of Jofeph given by Mofes, the reader will be able to form his own judgement. " When Jofeph faid unto his father, O my father, verily I faw in my dream eleven ftars, and the fun and the moon; I faw them make obeifance unto me. Jacob faid, O my child, tell not thy vifion to thy brethren, left they devife fome plot againft thee; for the devil is a profeffed enemy unto man: and thus, according to thy dream, fhall thy Lord chufe thee, and teach thee the interpretation of dark

fayings,

fayings, and he fhall accomplifh his favour upon thee and upon the family of Jacob, as he hath formerly accomplifhed it upon thy fathers Abraham and Ifaac; for thy Lord is knowing and wife. Surely in the hiftory of Jofeph and his brethren there are figns of God's providence to the inquifitive; when they faid to one another, Jofeph and his brother * are dearer to our father than we, who are the greater number; our father certainly maketh a wrong judgement. Wherefore flay Jofeph, or drive him into fome diftant or defart part of the earth, and the face of your father fhall be cleared toward you :' and ye fhall afterwards be people of integrity. One of them † fpoke and faid, flay not Jofeph, but throw him to the bottom of the well; fome travellers will take him up, if ye do this. They faid unto Jacob, O father, why doft thou not intruft Jofeph with us, fince we are fincere well-wifhers unto him? Send him with us to-morrow, into the field, that he may divert himfelf and fport, and we will be his guardians. Jacob anfwered, It grieveth me that ye take him away; and I fear left the wolf devour him ‡, while ye are negligent of him. They faid, Surely if the wolf devour him, when there are fo many of us, we fhall be weak indeed. And when they had carried him with them, and agreed to fet him at the bottom of the well, they executed their defign: and we fent a revelation unto him, faying, Thou fhalt hereafter declare this their action unto them; and they fhall not perceive thee to be Jofeph. And they came to their father weeping, and faid, Father we went and ran races with one another §, and we left Jofeph with our baggage, and the wolf hath devoured him; but thou wilt not believe us, although we fpeak the truth. And they produced his inner garment ftained with falfe blood. Jacob anfwered, Nay, but ye yourfelves have contrived the thing for your own fakes; however, patience is moft becoming, and God's affiftance is to be implored to enable me to fupport the misfortune which ye relate.

* Viz. Benjamin; his brother by the fame mother.
† This perfon, as fome fay, was Judah, the moft prudent and noble-minded of them all; or, according to others, Reuben, whom the Mohammedan writers call Rubil. And both thefe opinions are fupported by the account of Mofes, who tells us, that Ruben advifed them not to kill Jofeph, but to throw him into a pit privately, intending to releafe him. Gen. xxxvii. 21, 22; and that afterwards Judah, in Reuben's abfence, perfuaded them not to let him die in the pit, but to fell him to the Ifhmaelites. Ibid. v. 26, 27.
‡ The reafon why Jacob feared this beaft in particular, as the commentators fay, was either becaufe the land was full of wolves; or elfe Jacob had dreamed he faw Jofeph devoured by one of thofe creatures.
§ Thefe races they ufe by way of exercife; and the commentators generally underftand here that kind of race wherein they alfo fhow their dexterity, in throwing darts which is ftill ufed in the eaft.

And

And certain travellers * came, and fent one † to draw water for them; and let down his bucket ‡, and faid, Good news §! this is a youth. And they concealed him that they might fell him as merchandife; but God knew that which they did. And they fold him for a mean price, for a few pence ‖, and valued him lightly. And the Egyptian who bought him**, faid to his wife ††, Ufe him honorably, peradventure he may be ferviceable to us, or we may adopt him for our fon ‡‡. Thus did we prepare an eftablifhment for Jofeph in the earth, and we taught him the interpretation of dark fayings: for God is well able to effect his purpofe; but the greater part of men do not underftand. And when he had attained his age of ftrength, we beftowed upon him wifdom, and knowledge; for thus do we recompenfe the righteous. And fhe, in whofe houfe he was, defired him to lie with her, and fhe fhut the doors, and faid come hither. He anfwered, God forbid! Verily my lord §§ hath made my dwelling with him eafy; and the ungrateful fhall not profper. But fhe refolved within herfelf to enjoy him, and he would have refolved to enjoy her had he not feen the evident demonftration of his lord. So we turned away evil and filthinefs from him, becaufe he was one of our fincere fervants. And they ran to get one before the other to the door; and fhe rent his inner garment behind.

* Viz. a caravan or company travelling from Midian to Egypt, who refted near the well three days after Jofeph had been thrown into it.

† The commentators are fo exact as to give the name of this man, who, as they pretend, was Malec Ebn Dhór, of the tribe of Khozàah.

‡ And Jofeph, making ufe of the opportunity, took hold of the cord, and was drawn up by the man.

§ The original words are, Ya bofhra: the latter of which fome take for the proper name of the water-drawer's companion, whom he called to his affiftance; and then they muft be tranflated, O Bofhra.

‖ Namely, twenty, or twenty-two dirbems, and thofe not of full weight neither; for having weighed one ounce of filver only, the remainder was paid by tale which is the moft unfair way of payment. Al Beidawi.

** His name was Kitfîr, or Itfîr, (a corruption of Potiphar;) and he was a man of great confideration, being fuperintendent of the royal treafury.

The commentators fay, that Jofeph came into his fervice at feventeen, and lived with him thirteen years; and that he was made prime minifter in the thirty-third year of his age, and died at an hundred and twenty.

They who fuppofe Jofeph was twice fold, differ as to the price the Egyptian paid for him, fome faying it was twenty dinars of gold, a pair of fhoes, and two white garments; and others, that it was a large quantity of filver, or of gold.

†† Some call her Raïl; but that the name fhe is beft known by is that of Zuleikha.

‡‡ Kitfîr, having no children. It is faid that Jofeph gained his mafter's good opinion fo fuddenly by his countenance, which Kitfîr, who, they pretend, had great fkill in phyfiognomy, judged to indicate his prudence and other good qualities.

§§ Viz. Kitfîr. But others underftand it to be fpoken of God.

And

And they met her lord at the door. She said, What shall be the reward of him who feeketh to commit evil in thy family, but imprifonment, and a painful punifhment? And Jofeph faid, fhe afked me to lie with her. And a witnefs of her family bore witnefs, faying, If his garment be rent behind, fhe lieth, and he is a fpeaker of truth. And when her hufband faw that his garment was torn behind, he faid, This is a cunning contrivance of your fex; for furely your cunning is great. O Jofeph, take no farther notice of this affair: and thou, O woman, afk pardon for thy crime: for thou art a guilty perfon. And certain women faid publicly * in the city, The nobleman's wife afked her fervant to lie with her; he hath inflamed her breaft with his love; and we perceive her to be in a manifeft error. And when fhe heard of their fubtle behaviour, fhe fent unto them†, and prepared a banquet for them, and fhe gave to each of them a knife; and fhe faid unto Jofeph, come forth unto them. And when they faw him, they praifed him greatly ‡; and they cut their own hands §, and faid, O God! this is not a mortal; he is no other than an angel, deferving, the higheft refpeƈt. And his miftrefs faid, This is he, for whofe fake ye blamed me: I afked him to lie with me, but he hath conftantly refufed. But if he do not perform that which I command him, he fhall furely be caft into prifon, and he fhall be made one of the contemptible. Jofeph faid, O Lord, a prifon is more eligible unto me than the crime to which they invite me, but unlefs thou turn afide their fnares from me, I fhall youthfully incline unto them, and I fhall become one of the foolifh. Wherefore his Lord heard him, and turned afide their

---

* Thefe women, whofe tongues were fo free with Zuleikha's charaƈter on this occafion, were five in number, and the wives of fo many of the king's chief officers, viz. his chamberlain, his butler, his baker, his jailor, and his herdfman.

† The number of all the women invited was forty, and among them were the five ladies above mentioned.

‡ The old Latin tranflators have ftrangely miftaken the fenfe of the original word Acbarnaho, which they render Menftruatæ funt; and then rebuke Mohammed for the indecency, crying out demuredly in the margin, O fœdum & obfcœnum prophetam! Erpenius thinks that there is not the leaft trace of fuch a meaning in the word, but he is miftaken; for the verb Cabara, in the fourth conjugation, which is here ufed, has that import; though the fubjoining of the pronoun to it here (which poffibly the Latin tranflators did not obferve) abfolutely overthrows that interpretation.

§ Through extreme furprife at the wonderful beauty of Jofeph; which furprife Zuleikha forefeeing, put knives into their hands, on purpofe that this accident might happen. Some writers have obferved, on occafion of this paffage, that it is cuftomary in the eaft for lovers to teftify the violence of their paffion by cutting themfelves, as a fign that they would fpend their blood in the fervice of the perfon beloved, which is true enough; but I do not find that any of the commentators fuppofe Egyptian ladies had any fuch defign.

fnare from him ; for he both heareth and knoweth. And it feemed good unto them *, even after they had feen the figns of his innocency, to imprifon him for a time." Vid. Sale's Koran, vol. II. p. 34, & feqq.

Page 47, line 7, for fymytom, *read* fymptom.

—— 50, — 15, — *Korana* —- *Koranra.*

—— 58, 60, 61. Since the mountain Kaf is much celebrated by eaftern writers, the following defcription of it may be found interefting :

قاف or Kaf then is a fabulous mountain, anciently fuppofed, by the Afiatics, to furround the world, and to bind the horizon on all fides. In their writings, therefore, to paint the rifing of the fun, they fay, " When the ftar of day appeared from the height of Kaf, the world was enlightened :" whilft they exprefs the whole extent of the earth, by " از قاف تا قاف *Uz Kaf tau Kaf* From Kaf to Kaf." To account for the firft or falfe twilight (called الفجر الكاذب) which it followed by an intenfer darknefs immediately before dawn (named الفجر الثاني or الفجر الصادق The fecond or true crepufcle), the eaftern aftronomers fuppofed a window in Kaf, fome degrees below the fummit, through which the fun's rays being conveyed as he rofe, the world after he had paffed was left in temporary obfcurity till he appeared again above the horizon. Since, however, fome of their philofophers have applied themfelves to the ftudy of geography, they have difcovered Kaf to be Mount Caucafus, or Imaus, to the eaft, and Mount Atlas, to the weft ; over which the fun, in thofe countries, appears to pafs when he rifes and fets. In the Koran (for even Mohammed himfelf was carried along by this popular belief) Kaf his faid to reft upon a ftone called Sakhrat, formed according to fome learned doctors, of one entire emerald, the reflection from which, they fay, gives the azure appearance to the fky ; whilft its movements produce earthquakes, volcanos, and all the extraordinary phænomena of nature. On Kaf the eaftern poets and romances have fixed the refidence of the Dives or Genii, fuppofing them

---

* That is to Kitfir and his friends. The occafion of Jofeph's imprifonment is faid to be, either that they fufpected him to be guilty, notwithftanding the proofs which had been given of his innocence ; or elfe that Zuleikha defired it, feigning, to deceive her hufband, that fhe wanted to have Jofeph removed from her fight, till fhe could conquer her paffion by time ; though her real defign was to force him to compliance.

to

to have been here confined by Tahmuras, and the ancient heross of Perfia) : here, they fay, lies Jinniftan or Fairy Land; and here they place the city of Aherman (tne principle of evil), where Arfhenk, a genie king, they add, built a fplendid palace, in a gallery of which were portraits of the different kinds of rational beings who inhabited this globe before the formation of Adam.

The Dives, genii, or giants, in Eaftern mythology, juft mentioned, are a race of malignant beings, called likewife ديو نر *Dive nur* or male demons, the پری *Peri* or fairies, being fuppofed to be of the female fex, though it was imagined that both propagated their fpecies independent of each other, an irreconcileable enmity fubfifting between them. The Peris were, according to them, neither man, nor woman, nor devil; but anfwering in many refpects to that beneficent little being to whom our anceftors paid fo much attention, called the Fairy; which, from the refemblance of the name, and other circumftances, was, in all probability, of eaftern extraction. The old romances of Arabia and Perfia affert, that, in Jinniftan, they live upon perfume; and conceive them to be fo extremely beautiful, that they call a lovely woman پری زاده *Peri zaudeh*, born of the Peris. The Perfians fay, that four of the Dives, or malignant genii, made war upon Tahmuras, the third king of the Pifhdadian dynafty, by whom however, they were defeated, and imprifoned in frightful caverns; on which account that prince is called in hiftory and romance ديو بند *Dive bend*, the chainer or binder of demons. In the " Chronicle of Abujafar," there is a tradition, that God created the Genii or Dives long before Adam, and gave them the world to rule over for 7000 years; after which the fovereignty was vefted in the Peris and Dives for 2000 years more, under their fole monarch جان بن جان *Jan ben Jan*; but thefe beings difobeyed the mandates of God. Eblis, the devil, then an etherial angel, was fent from heaven to chaftife and govern them; when being joined by a confiderable party of malecontents, he gave battle to Jan ben Jan, and became in his ftead abfolute fovereign of the earth. Intoxicated, however, with his dignity, Eblis forgot that he was inferior to Omnipotence; to humble him therefore Man was created, and the proud angel commanded to obey him; but refufing; he was curfed of God, and doomed to everlafting torment. From this ftubborn difobedience, it is added, he was named ابا Iba, the Refractory; ابليس Eblis, the Defperate; and شيطان Sheitaun, the Proud: his original name having been حارس Hares, the Guardian or Protector.

ركايل

رکایل بن ادم *Rocail ben Adam*, Rocail the fon of Adam, according to Eaftern tradition, was the younger brother of Seth. Agreeably to Mohammedan tradition, his genius was fo extenfive, that Surkhraje, a powerful Div, who then reigned in the mountain of Kaf, fent to Seth, requefting the affiftance of his brother for the government of his dominions, in confequence of which he acted as his vizir for many years; when, perceiving, by his knowledge in the occult fciences, that his death approached, he built for Surkhraje, as a monument to his memory, a palace and maufoleum of fingular magnificence, where every office was performed by ftatues, which, by talifmanic art, difcharged all the functions of men.

As to اهرمن *Aherman*, he was the principle of Evil, in oppofition to اورمزد *Ormuzd*, the principle of Good. The old Perfian poems and romances relate many wonderful fictions concerning the mountain of Aherman, where all the demons were fuppofed to affemble, that they might receive orders from their prince, and then fly to the different corners of the world, fcattering difcord and calamity wherever they fhaped their courfe. Furdaufi, the Homer of Perfia, in his Shah nameh, defcribes one of his heroes, when going to fight with Aherman, as arming himfelf with all forts of charms and prefervatives againft his enchantments. This great work, the Shah nameh, or book of Kings, it may be obferved, was written about a century before the firft crufade; and it is not at all improbable, that fome difmembered paffages may have furnifhed many of thofe wild ideas of inchanted romance, which after that period overfpread the European world.

The Eaftern nations, carrying their ftrange conceptions a little farther, have imagined, that دامباک *Dambak* reigned over the Anteadamites. Thefe beings they fuppofed were flat headed, for which reafon they are called by the Perfians نیم سر *Neem fur* Half headed. Their principal refidence is placed in Moufham, one of the Maldive iflands, where they were attacked, according to the fame tradition, by Adam, from Serendib or Ceylon, and compelled to obey him. It is added, that they were afterwards appointed to guard the tomb of the father of mankind during the day-time (lions keeping watch at night), to prevent his body from being carried off by the Dives, whom they fuppofe to have been irreconcileable foes to Adam and his pofterity.

The above, it may be faid, are Perfian tales; but let us not ridicule them; they are dignified by Furdaufi, the Father of Perfian Poetry, as the mythology of the ancients was rendered important by the Homer of Greece. Every age and every nation have their fooleries; many received opinions even of modern times will

will not bear the touchstone of truth ; and the forcery laws of our own country are a far more authentic difgrace to human nature than all the wild yet pleafing fictions of the Eaft. Vid. Richardfon's Dictionary.

People tinctured with fuch fuperftitious ideas, it may be readily conceived, were eafily impofed upon by the defigning knave ; and aftrology, divination, and the interpretation of dreams, became fafhionable ftudies with perfons of rank and diftinction, for many ages before the Chriftian æra. It even became a cuftom to carry wherever they went, pocket aftronomical tables, which they confulted, as well as aftrologers, on every affair of importance. Amru , one of the greateft, and one of the moft penetrating of the Arabian generals, after having fubdued part of Egypt. and other countries, fat down before Jerufalem, and had almoft reduced it to furrender, when he was told by an aftrologer, that the predicted conqueror of the Holy City had only three letters in his name. Struck with this, Amru fufpended his operations, and fent a meffenger immediately to his mafter, the Khalif Omar , whofe name in Arabic confifts of only three letters : and upon his arrival in the camp, the town inftantly capitulated. Tamerlane feldom marched till the aftrologers fixed the lucky hour : and an ideot having once thrown a breaft of mutton at him, precifely at the time he was meditating the conqueft of *Kharemé*, fometimes called the *Breaft of the World*, he interpreted it, before all his army, as an infallible omen of his fuccefs. Much good policy, as well as fuperftition, may poffibly, indeed, have been at the bottom of Tamerlane's conduct ; as it muft have highly animated his troops, who were conftitutionally impreffed with the ftrongeft ideas of omens, fpells, and every fpecies of fupernatural belief : a moft cruel proof of which their anceftots had given when they over-ran the Khalifat in the thirteenth century ; for many of the Mohammedans having a cuftom of carrying about them verfes or chapters of the Koran, by way of prefervatives or charms, the Tartars confidered all they met, with fuch papers, as enchanters, and put them to death without mercy. The Tartars have ever, indeed, been fo ftrongly impreffed with the notion of enchantments, that we meet with ftrange details in fome of their moft authentic writers. Abulgaze, King of Kharezme, who writes a genealogical hiftory of the Tartars, very gravely tells us, that Tuli, one of the fons of Jengiz Khan, having been furrounded by the Kathay or Chinefe army, would have been cut to pieces, had he not ordered one of his magicians to turn fummer into winter. The conjuror accordingly began his operations, and continued them for three days, when he brought down fuch a ftorm of hail and fnow, that the Khan of Kathay's army, clothed in filken garments

M 2

ments

ments and thin ftuffs, being unable to move, were flangthered without refiftance. ---One Mahmoud, who pretended to be a forcerer, was followed by numbers ; and fomented a dangerous revolt againft Jagathai, another of the fons of Jengiz Khan, who fucceeded his father in Turkeftan. His generals marched to attack the rebels ; but, on the point of giving battle, the Mogul army finding themfelves enveloped by a thick fog, conceived it to be the enchantment of Mahmoud, and immediately fled, to a man. One arrow only, it is faid, was difcharged ; which, by a fingular accident, killed the forcerer ; yet fo ftrongly were his people impreffed with his fupernatural powers, that his brothers found no difficulty in perfuading them that he had only made himfelf invifible for a little while ; and affumed the adminiftration of affairs till his return. This revolt was afterwards quelled with fome difficulty *.

It is but little more than a century fince the conjuration of witches, demons, and fairies, was commonly practifed and taught in London by Lilly and others. Even the Hon. Mr. Boyle, (fee his works, vol. VI. p. 59.) and other men of great learning and found judgement, in other refpects, were ftrongly impreffed with a belief in thofe fupernatural beings, and of the power of fpells in commanding their fervice. In the Afhmolean Mufeum at Oxford are various formularies of invocation and incantations, collected by the very learned and fenfible founder ; who was ftrongly tinctured with thofe prejudices. See Afhmole's Collect. of MSS. No. 8259. 1406. 2. See alfo the Lives of John Lilly and Elias Afhmole, Efq. likewife Dr. Percy's Relicks of Ancient Englifh Poetry, vol. III. p. 213, 214.—Conjurors, witches, and forcerers, are accurately defcribed in our law books. Hawkins, (in his Pleas of the Crown,) fays, " *Conjurors* are thofe who, by force of certain magic words, endeavour to raife the devil, and oblige him to execute their commands. *Witches* are fuch who, by way of conference, bargain with an evil fpirit to do what they defire of him ; and *Sorcerers* are thofe who, by the ufe of certain fuperftitious words, or by the means of images, &c. are faid to produce ftrange effects, above the ordinary courfe of nature." All which were anciently punifhed as heretics by fentence of the ecclefiaftical courts, and burnt by the writ *De heretico comburendo.* See Lib. I. p. 5. By the Common Law, they could only

* Father Angelo obferves, that Magic is an art publicly taught by the Perfians and Arabians. He knew a rich enchanter of Baffora, a man much refpected, whofe fcholars were fo numerous, that they poffeffed one entire quarter of the city. At the found of a certain drum, accompanied by a kind of chaunt, they became, like demoniacs, fuddenly infpired with a real or affected phrenzy, during which they devoured fire publicly in the ftreets. This is a trick not uncommon with European jugglers. Thefe magicians, by way of diftinction, wore their hair very long. See *Garophylacium Linguæ Perfarum*, p. 155. Angelo went miffionary to the Eaft in 1663. See alfo Hyde's Religio Veterum Perfarum, cap. 18 et 19.

be pilloried. 3 Inft. 44. H. P. C. 38. But by Stat. 1. James I. c. 12. thefe of.
fenders are divided into two degrees : thofe of the firft degree, with their accefTories
before the fact, fuffering as felons without benefit of clergy. Thefe are of four
kinds ; " 1. Such as fhall ufe any invocation or conjuration of any evil fpirit. 2.
That confult, covenant with, entertain, employ, or reward any evil fpirit, to
any intent. 3. As take up any dead perfon's body, or any part thereof, to be
ufed in any manner of witchcraft. 4. Or that exercife any witchcraft, inchant.
ment, charm, or forcery, whereby any perfon fhall be killed, deftroyed, confum.
ed, or lamed in his body or any part thereof." And though a fpirit doth not
actually appear upon invocation, &c. or though a dead perfon, or part of it,
be taken up to be ufed, and not actually ufed, they are ftill within the ftatute.
This law, which would difgrace the moft ftupid of nations in the moft barbarous
ftate of ignorance, was not repealed till the 9th Geo. II. If we keep fuch circumftances in view, and pay a proper attention to chronology, when we read,
we fhall not, with any regard to juftice, look down with contempt upon the manners and beliefs of diftant times and diftant countries.

But at the prefent day too many perfons, otherwife of fuperior education, in
England, fupport a great number of cheats who pretend to tell fortunes. Thefe
people impofe upon the credulity of the public, by advertifements and cards, indi-
cating a power, from their knowledge of aftrology, to fortel future events, and to
difcover ftolen property, or lucky numbers in the lottery, &c.

The extent to which this mifchief goes in the metropolis is almoft beyond belief;
particularly during the drawing of the lottery ; where the folly and phrenzy
which prevail in vulgar life lead ignorant and deluded people into the fnare of
adding to the misfortunes which the Lottery occafions, by additional advances of
money (obtained generally by pawning goods or apparel) paid to pretended aftrologers for fuggefting *lucky numbers*, upon which they are advifed to make infurances ;
and under the influence of this unaccountable delufion they are too often induced
to increafe their rifks and ruin their families.

One of thefe impoftors who lived long in the Curtain-Road, Shoreditch, is faid,
in conjunction with his affociates, to have made near £300. a year by practifing
upon the credulity of the lower orders of the people.—He ftiled himfelf (in the cir-
culating cards) an " Aftromomer and Aftrologer.—That he gave advice to Gentlemen and Ladies on bufinefs, trade, contracts, removals, journeys by land or
water, marriages, children, law fuits, abfent friends, &c." And further, that
" he calculated nativities accurately."—His fee was half a crown.

An inftance of mifchievous credulity, occafioned by confulting this impoftor,
fell lately under the review of a Police Magiftrate, where a perfon having property

ftolen from him, went to confult the conjuror refpecting the thief, who having defcribed fomething like the perfon of a man whom he fufpected, his credulity and
folly fo far got the better of his reafon and reflection, as to induce him, upon the
authority of this impoftor actually to charge his neighbour with a felony, and to
caufe him to be apprehended.—The Magiftrate fettled the matter by difcharging
the prifoner, reprimanding the accufer feverely for his folly, and by ordering the
conjuror to be taken into cuftody "as a rogue and a vagabond."

But the delufion with regard to fortune-tellers is not confined to vulgar life,
fince it is known, that ladies of rank, fafhion, and fortune, contribute to the encouragement of this fraudulent profeffion in particular, by their vifits to a pretended
aftrologer of their own fex in the neighbourhood of Tottenham Court Road, who,
to the difgrace of her votaries, whofe education ought to have taught them the
folly and weaknefs of countenancing fuch grofs impofition, finds the practice of
it extremely productive *.

The act of the 9th George the Second, cap. 5, " punifhes all perfons pretending
fkill in any crafty fcience,—to tell fortunes, or where ftolen goods may be found,
with a year's imprifonment, and ftanding four times in the pillory (once every
quarter) during the term of fuch imprifonment. And the act called the Vagrant
Act, made the 17th year of the fame reign, declares fuch perfons to be rogues and
vagabonds, and liable to be punifhed as fuch †.

We cannot too highly extol the wifdom of our prefent legiflature in thus provid-
ing againft fo grofs an impofition, which was daily gaining ground upon the minds
of the weaker part of the people, particularly females, who were conftantly running
ning after thefe pretended wife ones, for information on various fubjects. But
furely the folly of the eaftern nations, which had its rife in the days of ignorance,
is not fo reprehenfible, as that of the more enlightened Europeans, who have for
centuries been reckoned the wifeft people on the face of the earth.

* The encouragement which this impoftor has received from the weaker part of
the females of rank and fortune in this metropolis, has raifed up others, who have the
effrontery to infult the underftanding of the public by advertifements in the News-
papers.
† Vid. Colquhoun's " Police of the Metropolis."

FINIS.

S. ROUSSEAU, ORIENTAL PRINTER,
WOOD STREET, SPA FIELDS.

NEW PUBLICATIONS

TO BE HAD OF

J. SEWELL, CORNHILL; J. MURRAY AND S. HIGHLEY, FLEET STREET; J. DEBRETT, PICADILLY; AND S. ROUSSEAU, WOOD STREET, SPA FIELDS.

1. RICHARDSON's DICTIONARY, Persian, Arabic, and English. 2 vols. Folio. Price 16l. 16s.

2. A GRAMMAR of the PERSIAN LANGUAGE, by the late Sir W. JONES. The Fifth Edition. Price 18s. Boards. 4to.

3. THE FLOWERS OF PERSIAN LITERATURE: containing Extracts from the most celebrated Authors in Prose and Verse; with a Translation into English: Being a Companion to Sir W. Jones's PERSIAN GRAMMAR. To which is prefixed an Essay on the Language and Literature of Persia. By S. ROUSSEAU, Teacher of the Persian Language. 18s. Boards. 4to.

N.B. This Work with Sir W. Jones's Grammar, bound together, 2l. 2s.

4. A VOCABULARY of the PERSIAN LANGUAGE. In Two Parts. Persian and English, and English and Persian. By S. ROUSSEAU. Price 7s. 6d. Boards. 8vo.

5. A DICTIONARY of MOHAMMEDAN LAW, BENGAL REVENUE TERMS, SHANSCRIT, HINDOO, AND OTHER WORDS used in the EAST INDIES, with full Explanations; the Leading Word of each Article being printed in a new NUSTALEEK TYPE. To which is added, an APPENDIX, containing Forms of Firmauns, Perwanehs, Arizdashts, Instruments and Contracts of Law, Passports, &c. Together with a Copy of the Original Grant from the Emperor Furrukhseer to the English East India Company, in Persian and English. By S. ROUSSEAU. Price 7s. 6d. Boards. 12mo.

6. THE PERSIAN MOONSHEE; containing, The Grammatical Rules, the Pund Nameh of Sadi, Forms of Address, Select Tales and Pleasing Stories, Lives of the Philosophers, Kowayed Us Sultanet Shah-Jehan, Dialogues, and some Chapters of the Gospel of St. Matthew, with Notes by the late William Chambers, Esq.—All in Persian, with English Translations. By FRANCIS GLADWIN, Esq. of Calcutta. Price 3l. 3s. Boards.

7. THE PERSIAN INTERPRETER; containing a Grammar of the Persian Language, Persian Extracts in Prose and Verse, and a Vocabulary Persian and English. By the Rev. EDWARD MOISES, M.A. 18s. Boards. 4to.

8. THE FORMS of HERKERN, corrected from a Variety of Manuscripts, supplied with the Distinguishing Marks of Construction, and translated into English, with an INDEX of Arabic Words, explained and arranged under their proper Roots. By FRANCIS BALFOUR, M.D. Price 18s. sewed. 4to.

9. A GRAMMAR of the ARABIC TONGUE, in which the Rules are illustrated by Authorities from the best Writers; principally adapted for the Service of the Honourable East India Company. By JOHN RICHARDSON, Esq. F.S.A. The second Edition. Price 18s. Boards. 4to.

10. A SPECIMEN of the CONFORMITY of the EUROPEAN LANGUAGES, particularly the ENGLISH, with the ORIENTAL LANGUAGES, especially the PERSIAN. By the Rev. STEPHEN WESTON, B.D. F.R.S. S.A. Price 6s. Boards. 8vo.

11. A DICTIONARY of the MALAY TONGUE, as spoken in the Peninsula of Malacca, the Islands of Sumatra, Java, Borneo, Pulo Pinang, &c. &c. in Two Parts, English and Malay, and Malay and English. To which is prefixed a GRAMMAR OF THAT LANGUAGE. Embellished with a Map. By JAMES HOWISON, M. D. Member of the Asiatic Society. Price 1l. 11s. 6d. Boards. 4to.

12. HADLEY's COMPENDIOUS GRAMMAR of the Corrupt Dialect of the Jargon of Hindostan (commonly called Moors;) with a Vocabulary, English and Moors and Moors and English. Price 10s. 6d. 8vo.

13. OUSELEY's PERSIAN MISCELLANIES, an Essay to facilitate the Reading of Persian Manuscripts. 4to Boards. 1l. 16s.

14. OUSELEY's BAKHTYAR NAMEH, or Story of Prince Bakhtyar. Persian and English. 14s. Boards. 8vo.

15. TOOTI NAMEH, or Tales of a Parrot, in Persian, with an English Translation. 18s Boards. 8vo.

16. CARLYLE's SPECIMENS of ARABIAN POETRY, from the earliest Time. 16s. Boards. 4to.

17. SCOTT's TALES, Anecdotes, Letters, &c. Translated from the Arabic and Persian. 6s. Boards. 8vo.

18. HISTORICAL VIEW of PLANS for the GOVERNMENT of BRITISH INDIA. 1 vol. 4to. Boards. 1l. 1s.

19. THE ALCORAN of MOHAMMED. Translated from the original Arabic, with Notes and Annotations. By G. SALE. 2 vol. 8vo. 16s.

20. WILKINS's Translation of the HEETOPADES of VEESHNOO SARMA, from the Sanscreet Language. 8vo. Boards, 6s.

21. ———— Story of DOOSHWANTA and SAKOONTALA. Translated from the Sanscreet. Sewed, 3s.

22. MAURICE's History of HINDOSTAN; its Arts and its Sciences, with illustrative Engravings, 2 vols. 4to. Boards, 3l. 17s 6d.

23. ———— INDIAN ANTIQUITIES; or, Dissertations on the Original Form of Government, and the Literature of Hindostan, Persia, Egypt, and Greece, 7 vol. 8vo. Boards. 3l. 4s.

24. THE ASIATIC RESEARCHES, printed Verbatim from the Calcutta Edition, with all the Plates, complete. By Sir William Jones and Others, 6 vols. 4to. 6l. 10s. in Bds.

⁎ An Edition of the above Work is reprinted in 8vo. Vol. VI. and some of the Duplicate Volumes in 8vo. may be had separate, to complete Sets.

25. AYEEN ARBERY; or, the Institutes of the Emperor Akber, from the Original Persian, by FRANCIS GLADWIN, Esq. 2 vols. 4to. 2l. 2s. Boards.
An Edition printed in Two Volumes, 8vo. price 1l. 1s. Boards.

26. GLADWIN's Dissertations on the Rhetoric, Prosody, and Rhyme of the Persians. 15s. Boards. 4to.

27. THE ASIATIC ANNUAL REGISTER; or, A View of the History of Hindustan, and of the Politics, Commerce, and Literature of Asia, for the year 1799. To which is prefixed, a HISTORY of INDIA from the earliest Ages to 1603. 14s. Boards.

28. ——————————————— for the year 1800. To which is prefixed, a Continuation of the History of India, comprising a View of the Commercial Intercourse between that Country and Europe, of the Rise and Progress of the Portuguese Trade and Establishments in the East, and of the Causes of their Declension. 14s. Bds.

29. Vol. III. of the ASIATIC ANNUAL REGISTER, for the year 1801. 14s. Boards.

7 6 3 5
n6

CPSIA information can be obtained
at www.ICGtesting.com
Printed in the USA
BVOW08s1320110418
513079BV00025B/905/P